the new

gardener

the new

gardener

ANTHONY ATHA, JANE COURTIER,
MARGARET CROWTHER, SUE HOOK
& DAVID SQUIRE

MARKS &
SPENCER

Marks and Spencer p.l.c.
Baker Street, London W1U 8EP
www.marksandspencer.com

Created and produced by The Bridgewater Book Company Ltd.

ISBN: 1-84273-634-5

Printed in China

NOTE
For growing and harvesting, calendar information applies
only to the Northern Hemisphere (US zones 5–9).

contents

introduction

Gardening is such a diverse hobby that initially the widely used range of techniques and terms can appear baffling. But it need not be so. Whether you have taken over an established garden or are starting one from scratch, this all-colour and thoroughly practical book guides novice gardeners through the complexities of selecting garden tools, draining land and testing soil. Other clearly explained techniques include choosing and buying plants, staking and supporting, using fertilizers plus protecting and rotating crops.

There is even information on the wide range of useful insects in gardens, such as those that eat the larvae and eggs of pests. An example is the adult ladybird which is able to eat fifteen to twenty aphids each day and up to five-hundred in its three weeks as a larva. Aphids, also known as greenfly, are those widely seen pests that suck sap from leaves and stems, causing general debilitation and yellowing. Additionally, aphids secrete honeydew which encourages the presence of sooty mould, a black fungus. Hoverflies – distinctive flies that characteristically hover in mid air – also feed on aphids, while beetles such as the violet ground beetle live in the soil and eat soft-tissued grubs and pests like slugs and the eggs of cabbage root-flies.

Paths, sheds and electricity

Creating strong, all-weather paths that are both functional and attractive is essential. The range of paths is wide and includes those formed of concrete, gravel and flexible pavers, as well as paving slabs. Whatever a path's nature, a sound foundation is essential to prevent early collapse; winter rain, frost and general flooding can soon destroy those that are poorly constructed.

A garden shed is an essential part of a garden; a haven where tools, lawn mowers, powered hedging clippers and other equipment can be kept dry when not in use. And, with the addition of a strong workbench and an engineering vice, general garden equipment can be repaired and maintained. Apart from cleaning tools after use and coating bright surfaces with a thin smear of oil, yearly maintenance of lawn mowers and hedge trimmers will greatly extend their lives.

Electricity in a garden is not to be considered lightly as a close combination of water and electricity is a recipe for disaster. Always have electrical cables installed by a professional electrician, as well as all electrical fittings in a shed or greenhouse.

Many pieces of electrical garden equipment are powered by cables, with sockets plugged into indoor power supplies. Always ensure that a circuit breaker device is fitted. Then, should a cable be severed by the blade of a lawn mower or hedge clipper, the power is cut off before it can cause harm to you. Incidentally, always wear boots or strong shoes when using a hover-type mower; additionally, wear protective goggles when using a chainsaw or hedge trimmer, especially if the hedge is full of dust.

Practical projects for all gardeners

There are many practical jobs in a garden that require special instructions if they are to be undertaken successfully. And this is where this all-colour and practical book assures success. With this book by your elbow every practical task can be undertaken with confidence.

The range of tasks detailed in this book is wide – from planting a tree to constructing a scented seat, which can be used to form a romantic feature in a cottage garden. Each project is explained, as well as the best way to tackle it.

After selecting the projects you want to feature in your garden, do not tackle them all at the same time. It is better to spread them over a couple of years than to construct them poorly and to become disenchanted. A garden should be for you and your family's pleasure, not a continual construction site.

getting started

Whether an established garden is being taken over, or a barren plot surrounding a new house is contemplated, this chapter offers a detailed and thoroughly practical insight into the basics of gardening. Thought is given to the selection of gardening tools; ensure that they feel comfortable and always insist on holding them in a working manner before deciding whether to buy. Additionally, this chapter is packed with a wealth of information that ensures successful gardening.

starting a garden

A garden is not only an extension of the house – it is also a blank canvas, or a piece of modelling clay, which you can use to create something that is unique. But with the huge range of plants and materials at our disposal today it can be difficult to know where to begin.

Elements of design

In making a garden you are juggling elements, built and growing, to get a pleasing organization of space, rhythm, perspective, colour, shape and texture. While manipulating all these ingredients you want to produce a harmonious whole – every garden needs to provide a sense of proportion and balance. The smaller the plot the more important it is to create an overall unity. At the same time the way you want to use your plot, the amount of time you have to spend, and also your budget, all come into play.

Golden rules

When thinking about how to design your garden you need first to bear in mind the type of soil you have, the local climate and the aspect of the plot. There are solutions for every type of soil and for sun and shade, but the first key to success is to go with what you've got rather than making difficulties for yourself by trying to impose shade-loving plants on a sunny garden or sun–

▶ *This minimalist garden employs strong hard-landscaping and design features. Perfect for a low-maintenance garden used for entertaining.*

loving plants on a cool, shady garden.

Then you need to ask how you intend to use your garden and what your general situation is. If you have a young family it will be going against the grain to have a rambling cottage garden or an immaculate lawn; if you have little time to spare there is no point in developing the kind of garden that needs constant attention ... and so on. If you want to use the space for living, perhaps as an area for entertaining friends, dining or even practising sport, rather than gardening, there are lots of ways of doing this too.

If you inherit a ready-made garden don't be in too much of a hurry to dig it up and start from scratch. Instead, live with it for a while to see what it has to offer in each season. And when redesigning, aim to retain any good plants or features and make the most of the garden's advantages. To see what plants thrive in your area observe other people's gardens and to get design ideas visit gardens that are open to the public and note effects that you like and how they are achieved.

▶ *Many different materials can link the garden to the home – reclaimed railway sleepers and gravel are a good combination for steps.*

◀ *The geometric lines of this formally planned herb garden are softened as the many different varieties begin to grow and billow out.*

General design principles

Certain general principles apply with almost any garden. The materials you use for paths, hard areas, walls or fences and screening, and for defining beds where applicable, should be in keeping with those of the house, and the garden should relate well to the house. It often helps to have a hard surface – from gravel or pebbles, bricks, stone slabs or even concrete – linking the house with the garden proper. Don't overstep the limitations of the plot and try to cram in more than will happily fit, and do select your plants to suit any constraints imposed by the nature of the soil and the garden's situation.

To make visual adjustments to the plot, use curves to disguise awkward shapes, open areas to make narrow parts of the plot seem wider, and thickly planted areas to narrow down a wide part. If a plot is long and narrow divide it crosswise to make a series of well-shaped areas leading on from each other.

▲ *You can liven up a simple family scheme with wacky furniture such as these sunflower-inspired tables and stools – perfect for young children.*

Safety and convenience of use are important considerations in any garden to be used for leisure, especially by families or older or disabled people. Potential danger spots include changes of level or direction, which should all be gradual if there is any question of special safety needs, and hard surfaces, which should have good grip and not be slippery after rain. Anything that looks as

though it could be used needs to be as strong as it looks. This includes posts which a child might climb or an older person lean on to rest, garden seats, which may need to be constructed so that they are easy to get up from by someone elderly, and fences, which may need to be strong enough to be hit by a football or run into by a bicycle. Water is an attraction in any garden but how to use it needs be considered with care as open water can be a danger where children are playing. A well-designed moving water feature, however small, is a delight for everyone who uses the garden for relaxation. Paths and openings should be wide enough, where possible, for two people to walk side by side, and certainly need to be wide enough for one person and a wheelbarrow. If a path leads alongside a border you need to allow extra width for the plants to spill over the edge of the border or the path will be lost in no time. A curving path can look even better if it curves around something such as a beautiful shrub, while a focal point, whether an ornamental tree or shrub, a stone birdbath, a piece of sculpture or a fountain can give the eye something to rest on and give a path something to lead up to.

Using colour

Colour is an essential element of the garden design, and although it will partly be a question of personal taste there are a few general rules about the effect that colours have used singly, as a backdrop or in combination.

Green – There are more shades of green than all other colours put together and it forms an essential buffer and backdrop to colours throughout the garden. Used on its own, it can be clipped and elegant, or lush and jungly, a calm and subtle range of forms or exotic blend of glossy leaves.

Pink – Pink may be rich and dramatic, as in the purple pinks and hot magentas, soft and gentle as in the middle range of rose-pinks or pale and sugary. It is best set against blues and purples.

Red – Hot reds are exciting and dramatic, but too much will give you the jitters, so tone them down with lots of surrounding, cool green. Exciting contrasts can be made with true blue and scarlet red or bright yellow.

Blue – True sky blue is one of the rarest of nature's colours, but there are numerous other blues ranging from cold, icy pale blue through lavenders to deepest violet. Blues in shade create a sombre mood, but look cheery and fresh if combined with yellow in spring. Darker shades suit strong summer light.

◄ Less can be more. This garden relies on well placed natural materials – rocks, gravel and grasses to create a calming impression.

Yellow – Yellows, like reds, are warm and inviting, but some are very strong and even brassy, so use these in moderation, with lots of green.

White – This is the most difficult colour to use well and white gardens can easily look either insipid or like a pile of dirty washing. But a white garden can also be sophisticated and elegant, especially if lots of architectural, green, large-leaved plants are used to create a lush backdrop. A good rule is to use only warm whites – those with pink or yellow in them, or cool whites – those containing a hint of blue or green. Don't mix them.

Making your design

While you are bound to want to make adjustments as the garden develops, having an overall plan to start with is important, especially where expensive materials and hard construction work will be involved, or budget-breaking plants that don't like being dug up and replanted. Start by making a rough plan of your plot, noting any good and bad points, such as shady and sunny, dry or damp areas, good and bad views, good shrubs or trees that you'd like to retain and the direction of the wind.

Use copies of this to map out rough ideas about planning and planting. Then, when you are ready, take the garden's measurements carefully and work out your final plan to scale on squared paper, marking out both position and eventual size of plants you intend to use and the position of all the construction features such as paved areas, steps, and garden divisions. We hope that this book will help by providing some ready-made solutions to a variety of real-life plots whose owners all have very different ideas about what they want from a garden. Seeing how these designs are made up, the plants our designer chose, practical projects for planting or building, and the alternative schemes that can be devised for the same plot should give you lots of ideas to borrow when you are planning your own garden.

◄ If you want a garden full of flowers, give some attention and pre-planning into how well the range of colours work together.

the tools you will need

Garden tools should be a pleasure to use, as well as being functional. Buy the best quality that you can afford and, if possible, always handle pieces of garden equipment before buying them to check that their weight and size suit you. Looking after your tools will ensure that they last for many years.

Digging and forking tools

❀ Garden spades – in several sizes, with blades about 27cm/11in long and 19cm/7½in wide border spades have blades 23cm/9in long and 14cm/5½in wide. Some spades have blades with tread-like ledges that enable more pressure to be applied by foot to force the blade into the soil. Most spades have 72cm/28in-long handles (the distance between the top of the handle and the top of the blade). Some are longer at 82cm/32in.

❀ Garden forks – for heavy digging and breaking down large clods of soil in spring. Also ideal for shallow forking between shrubs and herbaceous plants. There are several sizes: digging forks have four tines (prongs), each 27cm/11in long, while those on border types are 23cm/9in long. Potato forks have flat-sectioned tines about 27cm/11in long.

Hoeing tools

❀ Draw hoes – a 1.5–1.8m/5–6ft-long wood or plastic handle is attached through a swan-like neck to a sharp-edged cutting blade. Several uses, including forming shallow drills into which seeds can be sown, and severing annual weeds at ground level.

❀ Dutch hoes – a 1.5–1.8m/5–6ft-long wood or plastic handle is attached to a forward-pointing blade used to sever

◀ *Garden spades and forks are essential for digging the soil in winter, in preparation for sowing and planting in spring.*

weeds and to create a fine tilth. When using a Dutch hoe, walk backwards.

❀ Onion hoes – resemble draw hoes, but are only 30–38cm/12–15in long and are used to sever weeds around young plants.

Raking tools

❀ Metal rakes – sometimes known as iron rakes, they have 25–30cm/10–12in-wide heads, each with 10–14 teeth 6–7.5cm/2½–3in long. The wood or plastic handle is 1.5–1.8m/5–6ft long. Ideal for levelling soil.

❀ Landscape rakes – used to level large areas. They have a 72cm/28in-wide wooden head with 7.5cm/3in-long tines spaced 36mm/1½in apart.

Planting tools

❀ Hand trowels – a metal scoop attached to handle 15–30cm/6–12in long.

❀ Dibbers – they range in size and are used to make planting holes for cabbages and other brassicas in vegetable plots, and small holes for seedlings in seed trays.

❀ Bulb planters – ideal for planting bulbs in grass, they remove a core of turf.

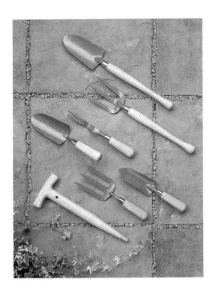

▲ *Trowels, hand-forks and large dibbers are used to plant small, ornamental plants as well as cabbages, cauliflowers and Brussels sprouts.*

Cutting and sawing tools

⚛ Secateurs – there are two cutting actions: the anvil type has a blade that cuts against a firm, flat surface, while the bypass secateur has two parrot-shaped blades that cross each other.

⚛ Saws – they range from Grecian saws (with a curved blade and teeth that cut on the pull stroke) to large saws for cutting thick wood.

Lawn tools

⚛ Rakes – from spring-tined types to rubber and plastic-tined models. They are used to rake debris.

⚛ Edging irons – often known as edging knives, they are used to cut lawn edges.

⚛ Edging shears – used to cut long grass at the edges of lawns. They have strong handles usually 82cm/32in long and shears about 20cm/8in long.

⚛ Hand shears – used to cut hedges as well as long grass.

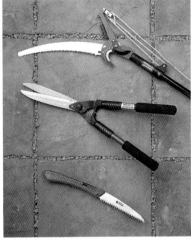

▲ *Essential tools for pruning and clipping are the long-handled saw (top), garden shears (middle) and hand saw (bottom).*

◄ *Dutch and draw hoes are used for weeding and forming seed drills, while edging irons are for straightening lawn edges.*

aspect and position

Look at your garden and see exactly how much sun it gets each day. Does it face north or south, east or west? South and west are best but many successful gardens face north or east. Which direction do the walls face? A south-facing wall enables you to grow a number of trees and tender shrubs.

Check on the sun

In an urban garden it may not be enough to see which way the garden faces. You may well be surrounded by office blocks or flats, terraces and tall buildings that shade the garden even when it should be in sun. And then how much sun does it get in the winter? Most roses, for example, need at least three hours sunshine a day for six months of the year if they are to repeat flower successfully.

That said there are a number that will flower in poor conditions, and even some that can be grown against a north-facing wall. You just have to check which plants will grow best in your situation.

Check the orientation

If a garden or street has been built running north–west or south–east, the gardener will feel that the garden actually faces north or south and plant accordingly. This can be a great mistake. In fact the side wall is the best spot and should be treated as a south wall because it will receive more sun during the day. Once you are aware of this you can plant shade-loving plants such as primroses on the opposite side of the garden, and they will flourish in the partial shade.

Temperature and shelter

Almost as important as the aspect is the temperature in the garden, especially in the winter and early spring, and the amount of shelter it provides. A small town garden may be an unlikely candidate for a frost pocket but if you are unlucky, the whole garden, or just parts of it, may be liable to frosts in the winter and early spring, when all around is frost free. Before the middle of winter frosts are harmless because most plants are dying back, and have reached their dormant stage. It is only in the spring, especially after an unaccustomed mild spell early in the year has started plants into premature growth, that a sudden hard frost can do major damage if they are left unprotected.

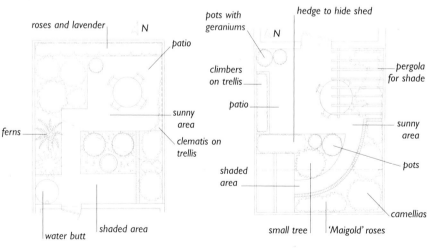

▲ South-facing walls enable the gardener to grow a number of climbers and trees that relish the sun, such as peaches and lavender.

▲ When the main part of the garden is in shade, choose plants with care. Camellias in tubs are good plants for shady areas.

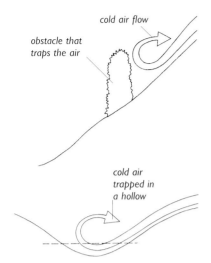

cold air flow

obstacle that
traps the air

cold air
trapped in
a hollow

▲ Frost pockets occur when cold air flows
downhill and becomes trapped in a hollow or by
an obstacle such as a dense hedge.

If your garden is seriously bothered
by late frosts then you must take care to
avoid semi-tender plants. The most likely
candidates are a number of early
flowering trees or shrubs, such as
camellias or the beautifully fragrant,
half-hardy winter sweet, *Chimonanthus
praecox*. Fruit blossom too, especially on
early flowering peach and apricot trees,
can suffer badly. If this is a rare
occurrence you may be able to cover the
plants when a late frost is forecast, but if
it is a common occurrence, only grow
plants that are fully hardy. Otherwise you
will be doomed to disappointment.
Strong, cold winds are another factor.
These can be a problem on roof gardens,
and you need to supply adequate shelter.

▶ Containers of lavender and geraniums for a
hot, sunny position in a rustic garden. The white
daisies help to emphasise the bright colours.

soil testing

There are many different types of soil, varying from county to county and even from one garden to another in the same area. The soil type is of real significance to the way plants grow, and getting to know the soil in your garden is a great aid to successful cultivation.

Soil is derived largely from rock that has been broken down over countless years into tiny particles. The size and type of these particles varies according to the type of rock from which they have been derived, and the way in which they were broken down. The other main ingredient of soil is organic matter. Organic means anything that has once lived – plant or animal remains. These are gradually broken down by a variety of organisms until they form humus, a friable, spongy material whose origins can no longer be identified.

Identifying soil types

Soil types are classified according to their particle size. The smallest particles are clay; slightly larger particles are silt, and largest are sand. The larger the particles, the larger the air spaces between them, and the more easily water can drain away. Sandy soils are free draining, but clay drains very slowly. Sandy soils also tend to be low in plant foods because the soluble nutrients are easily washed away, whereas clay soils are usually richer in nutrients and more fertile. Humus, because of its spongy texture, absorbs moisture and helps to break up tightly packed soil particles, making it the ideal soil improver for both light sandy soils and badly drained, heavy clays. In general, most soils are a mixture of clay, silt and sand in varying proportions.

▲ *Simply squeezing a handful of garden soil or rubbing it between the fingers can supply a surprising amount of information about its type.*

▲ *The varying proportions of the main constituents of soil can be seen at a glance if they are allowed to settle out in a jar of water.*

ADDING LIME TO SOIL

Most plants grow best in soil that is just the acid side of neutral, but vegetables may benefit from the addition of lime that reduces the soil acidity. This is largely because club-root disease, which affects brassicas, is less severe in neutral or alkaline conditions. Lime should not be added unless a pH test has shown that it is necessary; if the pH is 6.5 or above, lime is not needed. It is certainly not necessary to lime the vegetable garden every year as was once a traditional practice.

Carrying out soil tests

Dig up a small handful of soil from just below the surface and moisten it, if necessary, with a little water. Then rub it between your thumb and forefinger; if it feels gritty it is sandy soil, and if it's smooth and slippery or sticky it is silt or clay.

Now squeeze the handful of soil tightly then open your hand; sandy soils fall apart while clay soils hold their shape. You can also roll the soil into a ball, then into a long snake, and try to bend the snake into a circle. The more of these steps you can do, the higher the clay content will be.

Place a further trowel of soil into a clean jam jar, half-fill the jar with water, put on the lid and shake vigorously. Allow it to settle for several hours. The largest stones and soil particles will settle at the bottom, grading up to the finest clays, while the organic matter will float on the surface of the water. The relative depths of each layer show the different proportions present in the soil.

Take a number of soil samples from different parts of the garden and use a proprietary soil-testing kit to give a reading (full instructions are on the pack). The most useful test is for soil acidity (pH) because some plants will grow well only in acid soils. Tests for major nutrients (nitrogen, phosphorus and potassium) can also be carried out, but the results are not always reliable.

▼ Add lime to the soil only if a pH test shows that it is necessary. It may help to prevent club-root disease in the vegetable garden.

draining soil

Soil that is constantly saturated with water causes the roots of many cultivated plants to decay. There are, of course, some plants that thrive in moisture-saturated soil and they can be grown in bog gardens, but most garden plants need soil that is well-drained to 60cm/2ft throughout most of the year.

Checking if drains are needed

If water continually remains on the soil's surface then drains are definitely needed. Rushes and reeds are also signs of excess water, but the need for drains can also be established by digging a hole 1.2m/4ft deep, in autumn, monitoring the level of water in it through the winter. If the water remains within 23cm/9in of the surface, land drains are required.

Draining options

The options are rubble drains, clay pipes and perforated plastic tubing.

⊛ Rubble drains – relatively cheap to install if you have sufficient rubble available. Usually, only one main drain is needed with minor ones feeding into it, leading to a soakaway or ditch. The spacings between side drains depend on the soil: 3.6–4.5m/12–15ft for clay soil and 12m/40ft for sandy ones. Dig the trenches 30–45cm/12–18in wide and 60–75cm/2–2½ft deep, with a minimum slope of 1 in 90 towards the outlet. Fill the trenches about half-full with rubble, and place thick polythene over it to

prevent the soil clogging it up. Add soil, and firm it, until level with the surface.

⊛ Clay pipe drains – a traditional way of draining soil. Use unglazed clay pipes 30cm/12in long and 13cm/5in wide to form main drains, with 10cm/4in-wide ones as side drains. They are laid in trenches (as for rubble drains). In the base of each trench, form a 7.5cm/3in-thick layer of shingle. Lay the pipes on top and cover the joints with pieces of broken tiles or double-thick polythene. Over this lay a 10cm/4in-thick layer of shingle, a layer of strong polythene sheeting and then well-drained soil. Clay pipes are increasingly difficult to buy and plastic tubing has become more popular.

⊛ Perforated plastic tubing – quicker to install than pipe drains, this is corrugated for extra strength and bought in 25m/82ft rolls with a 10cm/4in or 7.5cm/3in bore.

Soakaways or ditches

It is essential to direct surplus water into a soakaway or ditch. If you are fortunate enough to have a ditch, allow the end of the pipe to extend into the ditch and

cover it with netting to keep out vermin. However, most gardeners have to construct a soakaway at the lowest point. Dig a hole about 1.2m/4ft square and deep; its base must be 30cm/12in below the lowest part of the trench. Fill to half its depth with clean rubble, then to within 30cm/12in of the surface with shingle. Cover this with double-thick polythene and lastly, fill up with soil.

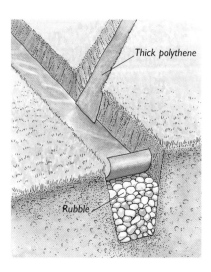

Thick polythene

Rubble

▲ *Rubble drains are relatively inexpensive, especially in a new garden and where a builder has left a mass of clean rubble.*

installing plastic drains

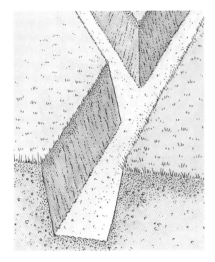

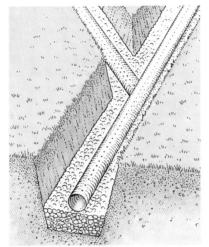

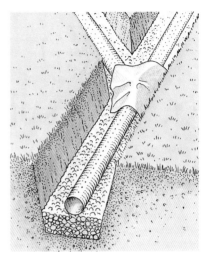

1 Use string to indicate the width and position of the main and side drains. Dig out the drain trenches, making a slight slope towards a drainage ditch or sump. Take care not to break the edges of the trenches.

2 Spread a 7.5cm/3in-layer of clean shingle in the base of each trench and lay the plastic pipe in the centre. Where each side drain meets the main pipe, cut its end at an angle so that they fit snugly.

3 Spread a double thickness of strong polythene over the joints to prevent soil entering the pipes and blocking them. Use a little shingle to hold the polythene in place while the other joints are covered.

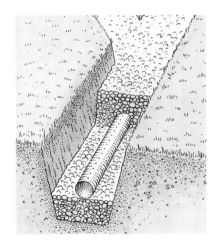

4 Cover all the pipes with a 7.5cm/3in-layer of shingle. Over this position a layer of strong polythene and then top up with well-drained soil. Slightly mound the soil to allow for settlement.

▲ *Well-drained soil is essential for most garden plants. If roots are continually wet, they will decay and eventually die.*

preparing the soil

Digging is a traditional part of gardening and is mainly performed in late autumn or early winter to prepare the soil for crops during the following year. Single-digging (to the depth of a spade's blade) is the normal way to prepare soil for planting.

Why dig?

Apart from making a garden neat and tidy, digging has several other benefits. It enables air and water to penetrate the top 25cm/10in of soil, and excess water to pass through to the sub-soil. However, if lower layers are impervious, water may remain on the surface. If this happens, install drains (see pages 20–21).

When the top-soil is broken up, roots are better able to penetrate the soil. Also, annual weeds become buried and perennial types can be removed. Digging also allows garden compost and well-decayed manure to be mixed with the soil. The process of digging usually leaves large pieces of soil on the surface and winter weather will break it down to a fine tilth by spring. Additionally, digging often leaves soil pests such as the larvae of craneflies and cockchafers on or near the surface for birds to pick off.

Single-digging

Digging is a systematic activity, and one that you will soon master. Do not dig too quickly, or for too long at one time.

As you progress you will find your own rythym and the work becomes very satisfying and relatively effortless.

Rotating crops

If vegetables with a similar nature are continuously grown on the same piece of land, it depletes the soil of the plant foods necessary for the healthy growth of those vegetables, while encouraging the build up of pests and diseases. Rhubarb and asparagus are permanent crops and are left in one position, but for other types of vegetables divide the plot into three and each year rotate the different groups of vegetables in the following order.

❀ Root crops – when preparing the soil, do not add lime nor manure. Instead, rake in a general fertilizer a couple of weeks before planting or sowing. Root vegetables include beetroot, carrots, Jerusalem artichokes, parsnips, potatoes, salsify and scorzonera.

❀ Brassicas – dig in well-decayed manure or garden compost if the soil lacks humus. If it is acid, apply lime in

late winter and a general fertilizer prior to sowing or planting. Vegetables include broccoli, Brussels sprouts, cabbages, cauliflowers, radishes, swedes and turnips.

❀ Other crops – dig in well-decayed manure or garden compost. If the soil is acid, dust it with lime in late winter and rake in a general fertilizer prior to sowing or planting. Vegetables include aubergines, beans, capsicums, celery, leeks, salad vegetables, marrows, onion, peas, sweetcorn and tomatoes.

NO DIGGING PHILOSOPHY

This has many advocates but is successful only where the soil is light, well-drained and aerated, and free from perennial weeds. Crops are grown on top of the compost regularly placed on the soil's surface. However, it can be expensive to buy compost each year, and where soils have a high percentage of clay there is nothing else but to dig, and to mix in well-decomposed compost or manure.

▶ *Digging flower and vegetable beds in winter improves the soil and makes the entire garden more attractive during winter months.*

single digging

1 The first step is to dig a trench 25–30cm/10–12in deep and 30cm/12in wide across one end of the plot of land. Move the soil to the other side of the plot.

2 Skim off weeds and grass from the adjacent strip of soil and place them in the trench. Additionally, add well-decomposed manure or garden compost to the trench.

3 Insert the spade's blade into the soil, at a right-angle to the trench and the width of a spade's blade. This will enable a block of soil to be easily removed.

4 Push the spade's blade into the soil and parallel to the trench; lift out the block of soil and place upside down in the trench. Repeat this along the trench.

compost heaps

Creating garden compost from kitchen waste and soft, non-woody parts of garden plants is an inexpensive and environmentally friendly way to feed and aerate the soil, and aid moisture retention. Compost can be dug into the soil during winter, or used as a mulch in spring and summer.

Making garden compost

Garden and kitchen waste can be just placed in a heap on the ground and left to decay, but this is not the best method. Instead, place it in layers in compost bins. Preferably, have three bins – one that is being filled, another that was filled months before and whose contents are rotting down, and a third with decayed compost that is being emptied and currently used in the garden.

Compost bins that measure 1–1.3m/3–4½ft high and square – allowing air to enter the heap without rapidly drying it out – are best. Proprietary types are available, while home-made bins formed of 15–20cm/6–9in wide planks of wood with 5cm/2in wide gaps between them work extremely well. Wire-netting bins can be used, but do line them with punctured black polythene to prevent rapid drying.

Filling a compost bin

Place a compost bin on a well-drained piece of soil and put a 23–30cm/9–12in-thick layer of coarse material such as straw on the base. Tread it firm. Then, add vegetable waste such as grass cuttings, annuals weeds and soft parts of plants, in a 15cm/6in-thick layer. When using just grass cuttings, make each layer thinner because thick layers become compacted and exclude air.

The next stage is to form a 5cm/2in-thick layer of garden soil. Thoroughly water it and dust with sulphate of ammonia at 14g/2oz per 1sq m (1sq yd). Alternatively, use a proprietary compost activator.

◀ *Circular compost bins made of wire netting are easily constructed. Line the sides with punctured polythene to keep the compost moist.*

Continue building up the layers and, when the heap reaches the top of the bin, thoroughly water the contents and cover with 2.5–5cm/1–2in of soil. Place and secure a plastic sheet over the top to prevent the compost from becoming too wet or dry. After about six months in winter (less in summer) the compost is ready to be used.

Medley of waste

In addition to soft garden plants, other materials can be added to a compost heap, including newspapers (but not glossy magazines), crushed egg shells, pea pods, potato peelings and tea bags. Do not use grass cuttings if the lawn has recently been treated with a hormone weedkiller. Additionally, do not add perennial weeds to the compost.

Mix up the waste as it is put into a compost bin because thick layers of the same material often prevent air entering the mixture.

Well-decomposed garden compost, ready for use

Decomposing compost

Compost bin currently being filled

▲ Use three compost bins in sequence to ensure a regular supply of well-decomposed garden compost.

LEAF MOULD

The leaves of deciduous shrubs and trees can be collected in the autumn and placed in 15–23cm/6–9in-thick layers in a compost bin, with a sprinkling of sulphate of ammonia between them. Leaves from evergreen shrubs and trees are not suitable, while leaves from poplar, plane and sycamore take longer to decompose than those from beech and oak.

Leaves can also be encouraged to decay by placing them in perforated black polythene bags (an ideal way to decompose leaves in small gardens). Add a sprinkling of sulphate of ammonia between the layers of leaves and, when the bag is full, add water and seal the top. About six months later the leaf mould can be used as a mulch or dug into the soil. It is an excellent means of reconditioning the soil.

▲ The range of proprietary composters is wide and includes this green design that is attractive yet completely practical for a small garden.

choosing and buying plants

Do not buy all the plants for your garden in one go. Since garden centres tend to stock plants flowering at that particular time, you need to visit on a regular basis, right through the year, to make sure your garden will have a continuous succession of flowers.

Ordering plants from specialist nurseries

The best plan of action is to make a list of the plants that you plan to grow and check if there are any specialist suppliers near you. Garden centres really only sell a very small selection. For example, if you want to grow a climbing rose against a north wall, then it is unlikely that a garden centre will stock a suitable variety. If there is a specialist nursery near you, they will provide a good choice, if

not buy one by mail order. Specialist nurseries are used to sending plants through the post, and they nearly always arrive in good condition.

Bare-root plants Always plant at the right time of the year, and this particularly applies to trees and shrubs. Generally they are best planted in the autumn when their growth is dying down but there is enough warmth and moisture in the soil to let the root system establish itself. Also, roses and

fruit trees are best bought as bare-root and not container-grown plants. This may sound a strange piece of advice especially if they are to be grown in a container, but plants raised in containers inevitably have a restricted root system and the bare-root kind, planted at the right time of the year, do better in the end. No reputable supplier would send out bare-root plants at the wrong time of the year. If you cannot plant trees or shrubs as soon as they arrive, dig a small trench in one

▲ *Always soak bare-root roses for a good half an hour before planting. Trim away any damaged roots and prune the stems lightly.*

▶ *A container-grown shrub for repotting. If the roots are congested, tease them out gently to allow the plant to establish more quickly.*

HEELING IN PLANTS

If you are unable to plant bare-root plants when you receive them, heel them in. Dig a trench with a sloping side, lay the plants in the trench as shown and then firm soil over the roots. These can wait until you have time to plant them.

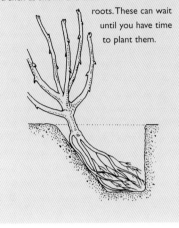

container, lay the plants in it at an angle of 45° and cover firmly with soil until you do have time to complete the job properly. They are unlikely to come to any harm if they are not left for too long. But do not let them dry out.

Checking the plants If you plan to buy the plants at a garden centre or nursery, there are a number of things to look for. Check the leaves for signs of pests or disease, avoid plants that have moss growing on the surface of their container because they have been in it for too long, check that few roots have grown out of the holes at the bottom for the same reason, and make sure that the plant is healthy with a good shape and equally spaced branches. It is worth taking time over each purchase to get what you want.

▲ *Garden centres are fun to look around and the plants in flower may well give you some new ideas. Check out each plant before buying it.*

▼ *The climbing form of the rose 'Iceberg' makes a graceful nodding plant. The honeysuckle helps to make a scented screen.*

using fertilizers

Plants make their energy from the sun by photosynthesis, but in order to carry this out, they need certain minerals that they normally absorb from the soil. These minerals are generally referred to as plant nutrients or plant foods. The three main minerals plants require are nitrogen, phosphorus and potassium, often referred to by their chemical names of N, P and K. Along with calcium, magnesium and sulphur, they are the minerals required in the largest amounts.

Other minerals are no less important but are needed in only very small quantities. These micro-nutrients or trace elements include aluminium, boron, copper, iron, manganese, molybdenum and zinc.

In good, fertile soils, enough essential nutrients are available for the plants' needs. In other soils, however, there may be a shortfall of one or more nutrients. This

can be due to the physical make-up of the soil, or to repeated heavy cropping that has used up the mineral reserves; it might also be that the minerals are present but not in a form that is available to plants (for example alkaline soils often 'lock up' micronutrients such as iron). Where the nutrients are not available in the soil, they can be supplied as supplements in the form of fertilizers.

Fertilizers
Fertilizers can either be straight (supplying one nutrient) or compound (supplying a mixture of nutrients). Details of which nutrients they supply are always given on the pack. The three major nutrients (nitrogen, phosphorus and potassium – always in this order) are the most popular ingredients of compound fertilizers, and the proportions are often expressed as N:P:K. A fertilizer labelled 5:5:9 is high in potassium, while one that is 30:10:10 is high in nitrogen.

The three major nutrients are the ones most likely to be in short supply in the soil, but other nutrients can be deficient too. Some fertilizers contain a mixture of both major and micro-nutrients, while others specialize in providing micro-nutrients only, and are often called trace element fertilizers. Sometimes the micro-nutrients are formulated to ensure that they will not be altered by the soil chemistry and made unavailable to plants; they are known as fritted or chelated compounds, and are ideal for alkaline soils. Some trace elements can be absorbed by the foliage.

◀ *Liquid fertilizers are fast acting and give a rapid boost to plants. Some types are formulated for absorption by the leaves.*

Natural fertilizers

Organic gardeners prefer to use all-natural fertilizers. Blood and fish fertilizer is high in nitrogen, with a small amount of phosphate. Bonemeal is high in phosphate, plus a little nitrogen. Seaweed is high in potash.

Methods of application

Fertilizers come in the form of powders, granules and liquids. Always read the application instructions carefully – some powders are applied direct to the soil while others need to be dissolved in water first. The application rate varies according to the product and the type of plant being fed. Wear gloves when handling and applying fertilizers, and keep dry fertilizers off the plants, especially the growth buds because they are likely to be scorched. Liquid fertilizers are less likely to scorch plants and are quick acting; they can be applied through a watering can or a hose-end dilutor for large areas such as lawns. Dry fertilizers can also be obtained as soil sticks or pills for easy application. Slow-release fertilizers give extended feeding over several weeks. They are normally granules that are gradually broken down to release the fertilizer, and require a combination of moisture and warmth to act.

▲ *Fertilizer granules: it is important to wear gloves when handling and applying any form of fertilizers and keep dry fertilizers off the plants.*

▼ *Fertilizer pills are now available for ease of application to soils where there is a shortfall of important nutrients.*

NUTRIENT DEFICIENCY SYMPTOMS

Nutrient	Symptom of deficiency
Nitrogen	leaves small, pale green or yellow, especially older leaves; growth stunted.
Phosphorus	leaves small, tinged with purple; older leaves fall early.
Potassium	leaf tips and margins turn yellow or brown, and look scorched; older leaves affected first. Poor flowering and fruiting.
Calcium	death of leaf tips and growing points; blossom end rot on tomatoes and peppers, bitter pit on apples.
Magnesium	leaves yellow between the veins; older leaves affected first, spreading to young leaves.
Sulphur	yellowing of leaves, first on young leaves then spreading to the whole plant. Not a common deficiency.
Iron	leaves yellow with dark green veins; young leaves affected first (unlike magnesium deficiency).
Manganese	yellowing and dead patches between the veins on young leaves.
Zinc	yellowing between the veins on young leaves; small leaves; browning of buds.
Boron	growing points die, leaves deformed with discoloured areas.
Molybdenum	distinctive strap-shaped, 'whip tail' leaves on cauliflowers.

staking and supporting plants

Many plants, from hardy annuals to fruit trees, need support. Those used to support ornamental plants must be unobtrusive, whereas for fruit trees they need to be strong, functional and durable. Here is a good range of ways to support plants in your garden.

Hardy annuals

Each year these plants grow from seeds and create spectacular summer displays. Many of them benefit from support.
❀ Twiggy supports – often known as pea sticks, they are cut from beech, hornbeam or birch trees and are needed in several sizes, from 30cm/12in to 1.2m/4ft long. Insert them among young plants immediately after their final thinning. Push them firmly into the soil, and use secateurs to trim their tops to slightly below the expected height of the fully grown plants.

Herbaceous perennials

These are plants that die down to soil level in the autumn and develop fresh shoots in the spring. Not all herbaceous plants need support but when they do, try:
❀ Twiggy sticks – like those used for annuals, but usually stronger and longer.

In spring and early summer, insert them around young plants. Many herbaceous perennials are self-supporting but others, especially those with a multitude of stems, require support.
❀ Stakes and string – an ideal way to support dahlias. Insert three 1.2m/4ft-long stakes about 23cm/9in into the soil to form a triangle around a plant. Then, encircle the plant with several tiers of string tightly looped around each stake.
❀ Metal supports – several proprietary types are available, one of the most popular having two halves, each with a curved top to form a circle, which encloses the stems.

▲ *Support sweet peas on a supporting framework tied with garden string, or with twiggy stick. Runner beans also need support.*

Herbaceous supports

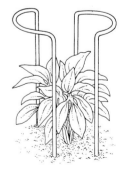

Sticks and string   *Twiggy sticks*   *Metal supports*

Trees

Strong supports are essential to prevent strong wind breaking branches and trunks. Choose from the following:

⚙ Vertical supports – the easiest way to support trees, whether ornamental or fruit bearing. Use a stout ash, spruce or chestnut stake that, when knocked about 30cm/12in into the soil, will have its top slightly below the lowest branch. Knock the stake into the hole before the tree is planted. Position the stake on the windward side using proprietary ties to secure the trunk and prevent it rubbing against the stake. This is the best way to support an ornamental tree in a lawn, allowing grass to be neatly cut close to the tree and its support.

⚙ Oblique supports – this involves inserting a stake at a 45-degree angle into the soil, with its top slightly below the lowest branch. The top of the stake must face into the prevailing wind. This is often used to replace a broken stake.

⚙ H-stakes – used after a tree has been planted. Knock two stakes into the soil, one on each side of the trunk, and secure a cross-stake to each of them, slightly below the lowest branch. Secure the cross-stake to the trunk.

Vegetables

Supports for vegetables need to remain strong throughout summer and with some vegetables, into the autumn as well.

⚙ Runner beans – use 2.4–2.7m/8–9ft-long bean poles inserted about 30cm/12in apart, in two rows 45–60cm/18–24in apart, with their tops inclined towards each other and crossed, making an inverted V shape. Position a horizontal pole along the top and tie in place. An alternative method is to use three or four poles to form a wigwam up which plants can clamber.

⚙ Garden peas – use twiggy sticks or large-mesh wire netting, 90cm/3ft to 1.2m–4ft high, held upright by canes.

⚙ Broad beans – insert a strong stake at the ends of the row, and encircle with strong string.

▶ *Herbaceous perennials with masses of stems can be supported with twiggy sticks pushed into the ground when plants are young.*

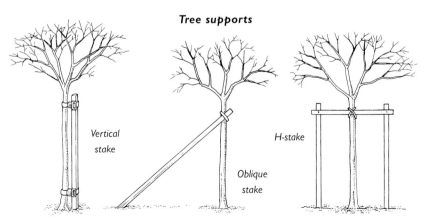

Tree supports

Vertical stake

Oblique stake

H-stake

sprayers and spraying

An efficient, easy-to-use sprayer is an essential piece of garden equipment. Pests and diseases are very common, particularly in the kitchen garden, and most gardeners are likely to find themselves needing to spray plants at one time or another. Even organic gardeners need sprayers, for they are used to apply organic remedies and fertilizers.

A sprayer enables a liquid to be applied as a spray of fine droplets, usually by forcing it through a nozzle under pressure. This enables the operator to achieve good, even coverage of the plant being treated. Where just a few plants are involved, a small, inexpensive hand sprayer holding about 500ml/1pt is sufficient. Although a small hand sprayer is useful for houseplants and treating individual plants in the garden, it has its limitations. It is often difficult to mix pesticides in such small quantities, and it is a nuisance to keep refilling the sprayer for larger jobs. Also, operating the trigger action is very tiring during prolonged use.

The next step up is a compression sprayer holding about 5–8 litres/1–1¾ gallons. Typically, this has a hand pump on top, and once the sprayer has been filled and the top screwed on tightly, a few strokes of the pump supply enough pressure to send the liquid through the nozzle in a fine, penetrating spray. This type of sprayer generally has a spray lance attached to plastic tubing to give a long reach. When the pressure of the spray starts to fall, a few more strokes of the pump are required to restore it. This type of sprayer is ideal for most medium to large gardens.

◀ *This type of sprayer is pressurized by a few strokes of the pump every few minutes. A long spray lance is a practical addition.*

▼ *A small hand sprayer is fine for occasional use, but is not practical where there are a lot of plants to be treated.*

For even larger spraying jobs, a knapsack sprayer is useful. This holds 10 litres/2 gallons or more of liquid and comes with straps so that it can be worn, like a knapsack, on the back. A lever on the side is operated with one hand while the lance is held in the other; the lever is pumped up and down gently and continually during spraying.

Knapsack sprayers are expensive and are only likely to be necessary for very large vegetable gardens or orchards, although they can be useful for lawns or treating large areas of vacant soil with weedkiller. When filled with liquid, a knapsack sprayer is very heavy and is unsuitable for those with bad backs.

Sensible spraying

The fine drops from sprayers can travel long distances on the breeze. Never spray on a windy day, when other plants or even neighbouring gardens could be unintentionally on the receiving end. Always follow the instructions for diluting and applying pesticides to the letter, and dispose of any unused solution as advised on the pack. The best times to spray are in the early morning, or in the late afternoon or evening when there is no strong sun to scorch the leaves, and beneficial insects are less likely to be harmed.

▲ *Knapsack sprayers are excellent for large-scale spraying jobs, but a smaller, cheaper sprayer is adequate for the majority of gardens.*

If you use a sprayer to apply weedkiller, label it with an indelible marker pen and set aside for this use only. Never use it to spray cultivated plants with pesticides or fertilizer as traces of weedkiller may remain, however well it is washed out, and could damage plants.

SAFE USE OF GARDEN CHEMICALS

- Store chemicals safely, out of the reach of children and pets, in the original packaging complete with instructions.
- Use the most suitable chemical for the job, choosing the least persistent type where there is an option.
- Read the application instructions and follow them carefully.
- Mix up just enough chemical for the job, avoiding surplus spray solution.
- Keep pets and children away while the spray is being mixed, applied and until it has dried on the treated plants, unless the label advises differently.
- Wash out the sprayer thoroughly after use, disposing of the rinsing water on to bare soil or gravel paths.
- Use gloves when handling concentrates and solutions, and wash all exposed skin thoroughly when spraying is finished.

protecting kitchen garden crops

Cloches and polythene tunnels are useful in almost every season in the kitchen garden, but never more so than when bad weather is threatening to damage crops. They keep off rain, wind, and a degree of frost; they can also protect plants from attack by a range of pests. In late winter and early spring they give early plants that little extra protection that will bring them on well ahead of the rest. Earlier still, they can be used to cover strips of soil required for early sowing. Keeping the rain off the soil will allow it to warm up and become workable much earlier than uncovered areas.

Tunnels and cloches are most suitable for low-growing plants, though with imagination they can also be pressed into service for taller crops. A pair of barn cloches, stood on end and wired together, are perfect around outdoor tomato plants to ripen the last fruits in the autumn.

Cloches

Cloches are made from glass or rigid plastic. Glass has the advantage of retaining heat better (like a mini-greenhouse) and being more stable in windy weather, but it is very fragile and dangerous when broken, especially in gardens where children play. It is also expensive, and makes cloches heavy and awkward to

▲ The earliest cloches were used for individual plants. Bell-type cloches are still available, but open-ended styles are now more popular.

▲ Lightweight polypropylene fleece provides young plants with surprisingly good protection against adverse weather.

▶ *The polythene tunnel is very popular with gardeners because it is cheap to buy and easy to use, though it has a relatively short life.*

STORING CLOCHES AND TUNNELS

At the end of their season of use, all parts of cloches and tunnels should be cleaned thoroughly before storing. Barn and tent cloches can be stored on edges stacked inside each other to save dismantling and rebuilding them, but take care to store glass cloches safely to avoid breakages and injury. Plastic materials should be stored out of sunlight to extend their life.

move about. Plastic cloches are cheap and lightweight, and not as easily broken as glass; they do not retain so much warmth and need to be thoroughly secured or they will blow away in even slightly windy weather. Cloches may be made from clear plastic, PVC, twin-walled polycarbonate or polypropylene. All plastic should have been treated with an ultra-violet inhibitor.

Early cloches were bell shaped (*cloche* is French for bell) or lantern shaped, and used to cover individual plants. This individual type of cloche is still available but larger cloches, used end-to-end to cover whole rows of plants, are now more popular. They may be made from two pieces of glass (or plastic) fixed together in an inverted 'V' to form a tent shape, or from four pieces of glass to form a barn cloche with its slightly sloping sides topped by a wide tent roof. The barn cloche is useful for taller plants, and can usually be ventilated by raising or removing one side of the roof. Barn cloches are generally made from glass held together by a number of wire clips, and are much more difficult to construct than tent cloches. Another popular cloche shape is an arc, made by bending a flexible, semi-rigid sheet of plastic, usually corrugated, and securing it with hoops.

To prevent rows of cloches from becoming wind tunnels, they should be fitted with end panels, which sometimes have adjustable ventilators.

Polythene tunnels

These are made from plastic sheeting that is stretched over wire hoops positioned over the crop. They are usually available as packs of hoops with a separate plastic sheet, but brands that have the plastic ready fitted over the hoops and which are folded up concertina fashion make erecting the tunnels easier. They are cheap, and easy to use and store.

Floating cloches

This is a term applied to lightweight perforated plastic or fibre materials that lie loosely on top of the crop, and are held in place by the edges being buried or staked in the ground. The material is light and flexible enough not to restrict the crop as it grows. Polypropylene fibre fleece is the most popular kind, and insulates the plants against cold and wind while remaining permeable to air and moisture. It tears easily but with care will last for several seasons, especially if it has strengthened edges. It is available cut to measure from a roll, in sheets, or as a 'grow tube' 90cm/3ft in diameter that is cut to length and used to fit over individual plants.

useful insects

There is a tendency to regard all insect life in the garden as potentially harmful to plants but not all insects are bad news – some are real allies in the fight against pests. It's important to be able to recognize who are your friends, because most insecticides are not so discriminating, and spraying and killing any natural predators will make the problem worse.

Beetles

Although some beetles are pests, there are many useful species. These include ground beetles, which live on the soil surface, hunting out insects, slugs and worms during the hours of darkness; rove beetles such as the scorpion-like devil's coach horse; and the familiar ladybirds (see opposite).

Capsids

Yes, some capsids are well-known pests but there are other species that are definitely helpful to gardeners. The best known is the predatory black-kneed capsid that helps control aphids and red spider mites on fruit trees. Similar in appearance to capsids are anthocorid bugs, another useful ally, especially on fruit.

Centipedes

Golden brown centipedes scurry over the soil in search of prey – insects, their eggs and larvae, along with small slugs and worms. They are often confused with millipedes (a pest) but millipedes are darker, have more legs that form a thick fringe down the sides, and roll up into a ball rather than running for cover when disturbed.

▲ *Slugs and worms may be dealt with by some useful kinds of beetles, although others are themselves garden pests.*

◄ *Hoverflies like to eat aphids and other soft-bodied insect pests and so are very helpful to the gardener.*

◄ The familiar ladybird has a voracious appetite, consuming huge numbers of aphids and other pests in its lifetime.

Both adults and, more particularly, larvae feed on large numbers of insect pests, especially aphids. A single larva can consume up to 500 aphids in its three-week life. Before emerging as an adult ladybird the larva pupates, and the yellow pupa may be mistaken for a Colorado beetle, which it superficially resembles. Ladybirds are most commonly red with either two or seven black spots, but they may also be black with red spots, yellow with black spots and black with yellow spots.

Hoverflies

Hoverflies could easily be mistaken for bees at first glance, though their method of flight is quite different – they hover almost stationary in the air, then make short, sharp darts forward. When they are at rest it's evident that they only have one pair of wings, unlike bees and wasps that have two. The larvae of the various species of hoverfly are very small, but most are efficient predators of aphids and other soft-bodied insect pests.

Lacewings

Lacewings are very delicate insects with pale green, almost translucent bodies, large, lacy wings and very long, constantly moving antennae. Both the adult lacewings and their larvae eat aphids; the larvae are rather insignificant, long-bodied creatures that are pale brown. Lacewings are found all round the garden, and are often attracted by lighting into houses at night.

Ladybirds

Nearly everyone can recognize ladybirds, but perhaps not so many could identify their larvae. While the adults are almost universally regarded as harmless, their small, armadillo-like, blue and orange larvae are likely to be treated with more suspicion, and are often destroyed 'to be on the safe side'.

Wasps

Wasps, as everyone knows, sting, and at the end of the summer they are a real nuisance, feasting on ripe fruit, and ruining picnics and outdoor meals. Leaving aside this anti-social behaviour, for the rest of the year they are a definite asset to gardeners because they collect all manner of soft-bodied grubs and insects to feed to the young wasp larvae in the nest. Other, less highly visible wasps are also extremely useful – several species are parasitic, laying eggs in the bodies of insect pests that hatch out and slowly consume their hosts. Ichneumon wasps are some of the best known, though rarely recognized in the garden. They have long, slender bodies and are not brightly coloured like the common wasp.

ENCOURAGING BENEFICIAL INSECTS

One of the best ways to help beneficial insects is to avoid using insecticide sprays if you possibly can, or to use only those that are specific to pest species and harmless to other insects. Leaving a rough area of the garden with piles of dead leaves and logs, and the hollow stems of dead plants, will also encourage a wide variety of insects. Specific crops can also be grown for them – hoverflies, for instance, will be attracted from far and wide by a patch of buckwheat in flower.

pollination

Plants reproduce sexually by means of seed. The seed needs to be dispersed as widely as possible, but the plant is at a disadvantage because it is in one spot. Animals and birds, however, can move about freely; one of the main ways plants disperse seed is by encouraging an animal or bird to carry it away. Embedding the seed within a sweet, juicy, edible fruit will certainly attract a range of creatures to help distribute the seed far and wide.

▲ *Apple blossom must be pollinated before a crop can be carried. It is usually necessary to grow at least two compatible varieties.*

The process of bearing fruit is therefore usually inextricably linked with sexual reproduction and the formation of seed. In order to form seed, pollen grains from the male part of a flower must be transferred to the stigma that is attached to the ovary, the female part of a flower, a process known as pollination.

Pollination is followed by fertilization when the male and female cells fuse to produce an embryo, or seed, which swells to form a fruit. If pollination and fertilization do not occur, the fruit generally (though not always) fails to form. When we grow fruit trees and bushes in our gardens, therefore, we need to make sure that pollination and fertilization of the flowers can take place.

Cross-pollination and self-pollination

Many flowers achieve pollination very easily, without the need for any outside help. Although there can be separate male and female flowers (sometimes on the same plant or sometimes on separate plants), the majority of species bear flowers containing both male and female sexual organs. Sometimes pollen can fertilize the female cells of the same flower (self-pollination), but often the flowers are 'self-incompatible'. This means that the pollen needs to come from a different flower, or different plant or variety of the same species (cross-pollination).

Many tree fruits such as apples and pears need to be cross-pollinated to bear a good crop of fruit. Some varieties are partially self-fertile so that a small crop will be carried even if no other fruit trees are nearby, but the crop will be greatly increased by cross-pollination. As insects are responsible for pollination, trees must be within insect-flying distance of suitable partners.

Pollinating partners

The two varieties of tree grown as partners must be compatible, and must flower at the same time. There are a few incompatible varieties; for example, 'Cox's Orange Pippin' will not pollinate, or be pollinated by, 'Kidd's Orange Red' or 'Jupiter'. Fruit catalogues give details and also have information on flowering times, dividing them into early, mid-season and late, usually indicating this by numbers 1, 2 and 3. Choose two varieties from the same pollinating group – for instance, 'Cox's Orange Pippin' and 'Discovery', or 'Worcester Pearmain' and 'Greensleeves'. Varieties from adjoining groups usually have sufficient overlap to be successful, but a variety from Group 1 will not pollinate a variety from Group 3.

Some varieties of apple and pear have an extra set of chromosomes and are known as triploids: they will not pollinate other varieties and need to be pollinated by two varieties themselves. 'Jonagold', 'Crispin' and

▼ Pear blossom: pear trees need to be
cross-pollinated in order to produce
a decent-sized crop of fruit.

HAND POLLINATION

In some cases, fruit tree blossoms need to be pollinated by hand. This is normally either because they are in flower very early in the year when there are few flying insects about, or because they are being grown in a greenhouse or conservatory where insect access is difficult. Peaches, apricots and nectarines are the usual candidates: they are self-fertile, and can be pollinated by blossom from the same tree. Wait until several flowers are open and the pollen can be seen on the anthers. Use a small, soft brush such as a make-up brush to lightly dust each flower, transferring the pollen from one flower to the other.

'Bramley's Seedling' are triploid apples, while 'Merton Pride' and 'Jargonelle' are triploid pears.

Looking after insect pollinators

Bees and other insects are very efficient pollinators of tree fruit. Make sure that you never spray the trees with insecticides during fruit-flowering time.

sheds, paths
and electricity

Garden sheds and paths are essential features in a garden, creating all-weather access and places to store tools and equipment. Sheds are also places in which vegetables and fruit can be stored, but they must be well ventilated and free from vermin. Electricity has become increasingly necessary in a garden and apart from powering lawn mowers, strimmers and hedging equipment, greenhouses can be heated by it. But it is essential that all installations are made by competent and experienced electricians.

choosing and erecting a shed

A dry, vermin-proof shed is essential in a garden to store gardening equipment and a wide range of paraphernalia. Always buy the largest shed you can; the average size is about 2.4m/8ft by 1.8m/6ft. Ensure that the site is level and firm.

Range of sheds

Sheds come in many shapes and sizes, some with a traditional apex roof (the ridge along the centre), others with a pent roof that slopes from front to back. A few have a combination of a pent roof and a greenhouse-like area at one end. There are also summer-houses that combine a garden room and storage space. Make sure the look of the shed suits the style of your garden, even though most are sited at the far end, especially if petrol or paraffin is being stored. Put it on a patch of poor soil or to hide unsightly features. You could even try to camouflage the shed by putting a free-standing trellis in front. You will also need an all-weather path connecting the shed to the house.

Most sheds are made of wood. Rigid PVA is an alternative, but it is not always considered attractive. Wooden sheds are made of a timber frame and clad with overlapping or tongue-and-grooved planks of wood. The type of wood influences the shed's price and longevity; softwood (usually known as deal and often fir or pine) must be pressure-treated

with a preservative, while more costly timber such as Western Red Cedar has greater resistance to water but does need to be regularly coated in cedar oil.

Erecting a shed

A firm, level base is essential. First, clear the area of vegetation and overhanging branches. Although the shed can be constructed directly on timber bearers –

usually 5–6.5cm/2–2½in-square and pressure-treated with a wood preservative – laid directly on soil, it is better to lay paving slabs. Mark out on the ground the area of the shed and ensure it is square. Use a builder's spirit-level to check the levels. Then, use 45cm/18in-square or 60cm/2ft-square flat paving slabs to form a base. Space the slabs 30–45cm/12–18in apart, and in three

rows. The timber bearers are laid on top, and at a right-angle to the timbers that secure the shed's floor.

If the shed is made of softwood, thoroughly coat all surfaces and edges in a wood preservative. Then, place the floor in position and re-check the levels. To enable the shed to be constructed quickly and easily, at least two – preferably three – people are needed. Screw or bolt the sides into position, holding each piece in position until it is secure. Then place the roof and secure it. Finally, cover the roof in roofing felt and use an adhesive to stick the edges of the felt together. The windows will need glazing. Non-opening window panes are usually secured by glazing sprigs (or panel pins); opening windows are more securely bedded in a layer of putty.

GAZEBOS

These are distinctive features that, by definition, let people 'gaze out' on to a garden. They have a long history and, in early Persian gardens, were descended from dovecotes which were positioned towards each corner. Gazebos create superb focal points when positioned towards the end of a large, broad lawn. Alternatively, position the gazebo towards a corner from where there is a wide view of the garden. They generally have a wooden framework, with wooden lattice-work at the back and an ornate roof. Simple ones can be formed from four stout, upright posts with a pitched roof. The back and roof are clad in lattice-work painted white.

◀ *Plant shrubs and climbers, as well as tall biennials, around a shed to ensure that it harmonizes with the garden.*

erecting a shed

1 The base of a shed can be laid directly on strong, timber bearers. However, laying paving slabs first and then placing the bearers on top creates a more substantial and frostproof base.

2 Ask a couple of friends to help you and put the sides and ends into position. These are either screwed or bolted together. Check that the construction is square and upright.

3 When the ends and sides are in position, put the roof in place. Ensure that the ends of the roof are firmly lodged in their sockets, and that it overhangs evenly around the sides.

4 Place the roofing felt in position: it can be laid longitudinally or across the ridge. Use galvanized, large-headed nails to secure it, and coat the overlaps with a roofing adhesive.

paths, patios and steps

Hard surfaces in the garden will stand a good deal of wear, but they do need regular maintenance to keep them in good condition. Spring is a convenient time to clean off the winter's accumulated dirt and grime, and spruce up surfaces; cleaning will also enable you to find and repair any damage that has occurred. The correct maintenance of paths, steps and patios will not only prolong their lives and improve their appearance, but is a necessary safety precaution. Uneven surfaces can easily cause people to trip, and on steps, this could lead to nasty injuries.

Cleaning

The first step is to brush the whole area with a stiff broom, paying particular attention to corners and under the overhang of steps where litter and soil accumulates. Use a paint scraper or similar tool to loosen compacted dirt in awkward positions, and to scrape out the gaps between paving slabs where weeds often grow. If a pressure washer is available, this is ideal, as it reaches into all the nooks and crannies with a high pressure water jet which has a powerful scouring action. Pressure washers can usually be hired by the day or weekend if you don't want to buy one.

Moss and algae are common where the surface is constantly damp and shady. Remove all traces of their growth; dichlorophen will kill moss and lichens on hard surfaces. Try to correct the conditions that caused their appearance in the first place. As for areas where dirt and soil have lain for a long time, they can appear discoloured when first cleaned. These marks can often be removed by a pressure washer or scrubbing. Other stains on paved and concrete areas, such as those caused by oil, can be more difficult to tackle. There are various proprietary products available, or you could try mixing a spirit (such as paint thinner) with sawdust until the sawdust is thoroughly dampened, and apply this in a thick layer over the stain. Sweep it off with a stiff broom and repeat until successful.

Incidentally, concrete will have a longer life if it is coated with a waterproof sealant. Special products are available for applying to old concrete.

◀ *Before any repairs on slabs or concrete are attempted, all loose material must be removed by using a wire brush.*

Repairs

Paving slabs may have settled unevenly to create protruding edges which can trip people up. Where necessary the uneven slabs should be removed, the base levelled and the slabs relaid.

Isolated cracks in concrete or slabs can be repaired. Use a hammer and chisel to chip along each side of the crack to neaten it, then wire brush the crack thoroughly to remove all the loose material. Coat the sides with a proprietary bonding agent before filling the crack with mortar or a patching compound.

Concrete pigments can be mixed with the mortar to help match the surface colour, and make the repair less obvious.

▲ Sometimes it is necessary to use a hammer and chisel along the sides of the crack to open it out before it can be repaired.

Concrete areas may look unsightly because poor workmanship when they were laid has caused the surface to wear badly, so it is pockmarked with shallow holes. As long as the base is sound, the top can be resurfaced, but the new layer must be at least 5cm/2in thick to prevent it from flaking away. The worn surface must be cleaned thoroughly and coated with a bonding agent before a sand and cement mix is applied. Resurfacing is often only a temporary solution; complete replacement of the concrete may eventually be needed.

SAFETY PRECAUTIONS

- Wear eye protection when using a chisel and hammer to work on hard surfaces, or to break up slabs.
- Take care to avoid back strain when trying to prise up or lift slabs – two people make the job much easier than one.
- Wear a mask when working with dry cement to prevent breathing in the dust.
- Protect your skin when handling concrete and mortar; always wear gloves to prevent irritation.

◀ Fill in the prepared crack with mortar or a patching compound, smoothing it out carefully to keep the surface level.

electricity in a garden

Electric power in a garden means you can use a wide range of equipment, including heated propagation units in greenhouses, lights in sheds, fountains in ponds and decorative lights on a patio. But you must ensure that it is correctly and safely installed by a professional electrician.

Lights on a patio

Warm summer evenings provide the perfect opportunity to linger on patios, especially if lighting is installed. Lights are also a good way of deterring burglars, especially if an infra-red

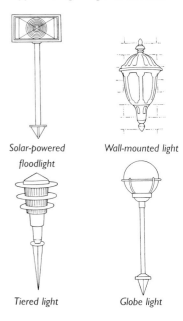

Types of lighting installation

Solar-powered floodlight

Wall-mounted light

Tiered light

Globe light

◄ *Garden ponds, with spotlights illuminating fountains and subdued lighting on other areas, are attractive in the evenings.*

detector (PIR) is attached. This works when it is dark and responds to body heat by turning on the light. A PIR can also be fitted to a spotlight circuit at the front of a house to illuminate a drive or path, but make sure it will not be activated by people walking on a nearby pavement, otherwise it may be going on and off all night. The range of patio lights is wide and includes low-level spotlights and those mounted on the tops, sides and bases of walls. Some can even be placed in patio borders.

Pond power

In ponds there are two choices of power – mains electricity at 240 volts and low-voltage power at 12 or 24 volts. In most areas in a garden, from patios to greenhouses and garden sheds, mains electricity is best because it provides strong lighting and power, but in or near ponds many gardeners prefer the safer 12 or 24 volt supply (a transformer reduces the power) for lights and a small fountain. However, where the demand is for several fountains, a waterfall and strong lighting, 240 volts is definitely needed, but note that it is far more expensive to install mains supply than low voltage. You can also buy solar-powered fountains that are easy to install, but they do need sunshine to work.

Greenhouse power

Mains electricity at 240 volts is ideal in greenhouses, especially where electrical tubular heaters are installed. Fan heaters also need this power, as do propagation

units. Small mist-propagation units are now available for amateur greenhouses, and they too require 240 volts.

Have the power installed by a competent electrician, with a mains board fitted near the door and at least 1.2m/4ft above the ground. Tack a loose sheet of plastic over it to keep off water droplets, but ensure that there is good air circulation around it. Additionally, have a Residual Current Device (RCD) fitted into the circuit to cut off the power if a fault occurs.

Power in sheds

This is not essential but it makes life easier, especially in winter when lawn mowers and other equipment need servicing. Ensure a mains board is fitted, so that it can be isolated from the house.

▲ *Lights at ground level and flush with the surface are ideal for illuminating plants around paved areas. Plants in containers can be placed on top.*

seeds, cuttings and dividing plants

Increasing plants, perhaps by sowing seeds, taking cuttings or through division, is a desire of most gardeners. Few gardening activities create the excitement and anticipation of taking cuttings and waiting for them to develop roots. And most forms of propagation do not require additional warmth — hardy annuals are sown in spring directly into a border, as well as many vegetables. And all that is needed is several packets of seeds. Some cuttings, however, benefit from the provision of gentle warmth.

sowing seeds – handy tips

Fine seeds should be sown as thinly as possible. Take care and time when sowing to achieve this. There isn't any point in filling a seed tray with a large number of seeds, for when they all germinate, the tray is too congested, the seedlings don't grow properly, and it is difficult to prick them out.

Sowing larger seeds

They are much easier to sow and generally include vegetables, i.e. peas and beans, although clivias have lovely dark brown seeds that in two year's time make excellent and unusual presents.

If you plan to grow vegetables in your container garden then it is a good idea to sow them separately, and you should plan to operate on the two-for-one principle. Sow peas and beans, for example, in degradable cardboard pots or modules, two seeds at a time and discard one if both germinate. Then plant the pot or module directly into the container in early summer when all danger of frost has passed. The plants will then grow without suffering any check.

Watering

Try to water seed pans and small seedlings from below, rather than from above. It is very difficult to get a fine enough rose spray, and the heavy drops of water damage the seedlings and can even wash out the roots. Stand the trays in a tray of water and the compost will absorb sufficient water to keep the seeds damp and the small plants growing.

Temperature

Every seed has a temperature at which it will germinate, and it is particularly important to stick to this. It will be stated on the seed packet. Nearly all vegetables require a soil temperature of above 7°C/45°F for a week before they germinate, and a number of annuals require temperatures from 13°–21°C/55°–70°F. Read the instructions carefully on the packet.

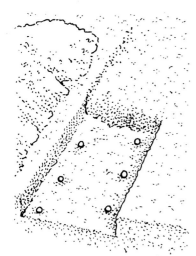

▲ *Larger seeds, such as peas and beans, can be sown in shallow double trenches. Space them out according to packet instructions.*

SOWING SEED DIRECTLY INTO THE CONTAINER

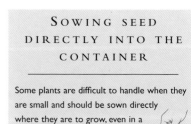

Some plants are difficult to handle when they are small and should be sown directly where they are to grow, even in a container. This applies to a number of vegetables such as carrots, beetroot and chives. Thin the seedlings when they appear. Hardy annuals are often sown in this way in the kitchen garden, and if you have a container devoted to hardy annuals you can follow this practice. Draw shapes on the surface of the container, and then sow individual plants in each section. Sow the seed thinly. Borage, flax, Californian poppy, *Eschscholzia*, and poached egg plant, *Limnanthes*, can all be sown in this way.

Aftercare

The worst thing that can happen to a tray of seedlings is the fungal disease called 'damping off'. This usually happens when seedlings are too crowded within the seed tray, or when the compost itself is too cold and too wet.

Spray the seedlings from time to time with a fungicide as a prevention, and take care to keep all containers that you use as clean as you possibly can. And do not forget to turn the seed trays on windowsills every day or the plants will grow lopsided towards the light. Put them outside as soon as possible, shade them from direct sunlight to start with, and water them with a diluted liquid fertiliser every week.

▲ Growing peas in a container is most satisfying; train the plants up a wigwam of canes. Choose a mangetout variety.

▼ It is a help when raising annuals from seed to stick to one colour, as this can then be matched with other plants in beds and pots.

propagation – taking cuttings

There is something very satisfying about taking cuttings and propagating your own plants. It is actually very simple and the principle is invariably the same – cut off a portion of the parent plant, dip the cutting in hormone rooting powder, and replant it in moist compost.

Softwood cuttings

They are taken in the spring when the new shoots are fully formed and are just starting to harden. They are usually taken from the tips of new shoots but with some plants the cuttings are taken from new basal shoots, growing from the base of the plant. Make the cut just below a node (a leaf joint), and then reduce the number of leaves and the leaf area by cutting some of the leaves in half. Cuttings require some leaf growth but find it difficult to support a large leaf system. Dip the cutting in hormone rooting powder and push the cutting into moist compost. It is very important to keep softwood cuttings in a moist environment, preferably a propagating frame because they lose moisture quickly.

Semi-ripe cuttings

They are taken in late summer from new wood produced in the current year.

▶ *Geraniums are easily raised from cuttings and can be overwintered on windowsills or in a cool greenhouse. This is a great money saver!*

▶ *Osteospermums are easily raised from softwood cuttings taken early in the year. The variety 'Whirligig' has wheel-like petals.*

Choose a non-flowering shoot if available. Cuttings 5–10cm/2–4in long are about the normal length. Trim them just below a leaf joint and remove the lower leaves. Remove the top leaves to reduce moisture loss. Dip the cutting in rooting powder and insert it gently into the cutting compost.

Some shrubs and herbs root best from semi-ripe cuttings taken with a 'heel' of the old wood. Pull the shoot

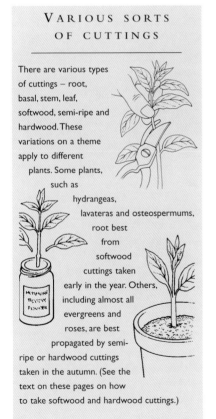

VARIOUS SORTS OF CUTTINGS

There are various types of cuttings – root, basal, stem, leaf, softwood, semi-ripe and hardwood. These variations on a theme apply to different plants. Some plants, such as hydrangeas, lavateras and osteospermums, root best from softwood cuttings taken early in the year. Others, including almost all evergreens and roses, are best propagated by semi-ripe or hardwood cuttings taken in the autumn. (See the text on these pages on how to take softwood and hardwood cuttings.)

away from the plant in a downwards direction and it will come away with a heel of wood. Trim this if necessary.

Stem cuttings

Most hardwood and semi-ripe cuttings are stem cuttings taken from a straight length of shoot. The normal length is around 5–12cm/2–5in. Trim each stem to length just below a node, and strip away the lower leaves to allow the shoot to be inserted in the compost. Also remove all flowering shoots and buds because they reduce the effect of the

root-producing hormones that cuttings rely on. Pelargoniums are normally propagated from stem cuttings, as are a number of other plants. In fact, pelargoniums are a good example of those plants that need to be left in the open air overnight to form a pad at the foot of the stem. In some plants this helps rooting, in others it helps to prevent the cuttings rotting. If you have difficulty in getting pelargoniums to root then this is worth trying. Dip all cuttings in hormone rooting powder, or a hormone rooting solution.

cuttings and division

Division

Many plants, especially perennials that have spreading rootstocks, can easily be propagated by division in spring. This is something that all gardeners should practise because some plants, such as delphiniums, form large clumps of roots where the centre dies away. Such plants should be split and only the healthy outer sections of the roots replanted.

Primroses, hostas, irises and pulmonarias should all be divided in this way. There are two schools of thought about how this should be done. Some plants, such as primroses, can simply be pulled apart and the various portions replanted. Other fibrous-rooted plants have to be split by cutting through the rootball with a spade, or pulling the plant apart, using two forks back to back. It is best to split

the rootball cleanly with a spade or a sharp knife.

Leaf cuttings

This is the simplest form of propagation and is normally used for house plants, such as streptocarpus and African violet, *Saintpaulia*. Some plants root best when a whole leaf is used, pinned out flat on the compost, with a few small cuts or nicks made in the veins on the underside of the leaf. This encourages the plants to form calluses and the roots spring from them (begonias are often propagated in this way). Another common house plant

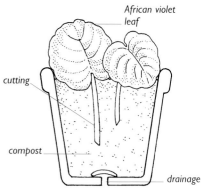

African violet leaf

cutting

compost

drainage

▲ *African violets are easy to propagate by leaf cuttings. Pull off a number of leaves and insert them in compost around the edge of the pot.*

◀ *Make sure the base of the leaf is touching the surface of the compost. New leaves will show in a few weeks.*

dividing plants successfully

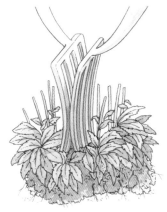

1 Some smaller plants, such as primroses and pulmonarias, can be divided easily by hand. Dig up the plant when flowering is over and pull it apart.

2 Large perennials can be divided with two forks, as shown. Put the forks in back to back and lever the plant apart. Or, just cut the plant in two with a spade.

3 Irises can be divided, cutting the new rhizomes away from the old clump. Dust with fungicide powder and cut back the leaves by two-thirds before replanting.

propagated by leaf cuttings is the African violet. Pull off whole leaves including the stalk and push them into compost around the rim of a pot. Some may not take but others will. Streptocarpus is best propagated by cutting the leaf into strips and then planting them in compost, edge down.

Layering This occurs naturally in many plants, and the method can be used to propagate a number of plants that are difficult to raise from cuttings, such as rhododendrons. Strawberries propagate themselves by sending out runners that root. They can then be severed from the parent plant and potted up separately. Blackberries propagate themselves by tip-layering where the tips of shoots bury themselves in the ground and

develop roots. This is the principle behind layering. Peg a branch of a plant or shrub down, burying part of it in the ground. You can nick the stem lightly to promote rooting if you wish. Serpentine layering is where a long branch is pegged down in waves with the crests above ground. This can produce several plants from one stem.

General points when taking cuttings
Choose shoots without flowers or flowering buds if possible: non-flowering shoots produce roots more quickly. Use a sharp knife and make your cuts cleanly between or just below a node. Keep all cuttings moist and use a propagating frame for softwood cuttings. Leave hardwood cuttings in the ground for one year. They are generally slow to take.

HARDWOOD CUTTINGS

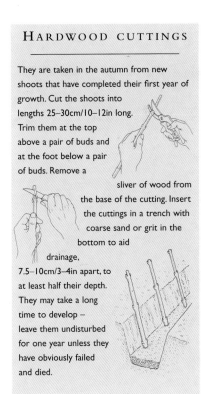

They are taken in the autumn from new shoots that have completed their first year of growth. Cut the shoots into lengths 25–30cm/10–12in long. Trim them at the top above a pair of buds and at the foot below a pair of buds. Remove a sliver of wood from the base of the cutting. Insert the cuttings in a trench with coarse sand or grit in the bottom to aid drainage, 7.5–10cm/3–4in apart, to at least half their depth. They may take a long time to develop – leave them undisturbed for one year unless they have obviously failed and died.

potting, planting and feeding

Potting, planting and feeding are regular jobs when looking after plants. Planting a plant so that its roots are spread out and in close contact with the soil is essential to encourage rapid establishment and subsequent growth. Additionally, cuttings and young seedlings sown in greenhouses require potting-up, and established plants in pots often need regular transfer to larger pots and thereby more compost. Ensuring plants have a healthy and balanced diet is also important.

potting and repotting

Don't be put off by technical planting terms. Potting up means transferring a young seedling into its first pot; repotting means taking the plant out of the container and then replanting it in the same container with new compost; and potting on means transferring a plant to a larger container.

◄ *When a plant outgrows its container, pot it on into a container that is approximately 5cm/2in larger than the present one.*

The general principles of planting

All plants must be planted in containers large enough to accommodate their root systems. The container should be 5cm/2in larger than the rootball of the plant. To plant a shrub remove it from the original container and gently tease out the roots if they have become congested, and trim off any damaged roots. Put a good layer of crocks, broken tiles or stones at the bottom of the new container to provide adequate drainage, and then add a layer of compost. Put the plant in the container, making certain that the soil level is the same in the new container as it was in the old. Check the soil mark on the plant to do this accurately. Add compost around the sides of the pot making sure that it is pressed firmly against the roots. Firm the soil with your hands or a dibber, but do not ram the compost down too tightly. Lift the container, if you can, and rap it

repotting a plant

1 Put a handful of broken crocks or small stones in the bottom of any container. This prevents the compost draining away when the plant is watered.

2 Remove the plant carefully from the old container. Check the soil level. The plant should be replanted at the same depth in the new container.

3 Tease out the roots if they have become congested and trim away any that are damaged. This helps them to spread out into the new compost.

down on a hard surface two or three times to shake out any air pockets. Finally, water thoroughly and top up the level with compost as it settles. To save moving a heavy pot into position, site it where you need it before starting.

Potting on Young plants need to be transferred from small pots to larger pots, depending on their rate of growth. This should be done carefully. Transfer a growing plant to a pot just larger than the existing one, say by about 5cm/2in. This helps to keep the plant growing at a steady rate – if you potted on into a much larger pot, the roots would spread out too quickly, upsetting the growth balance. If a plant is slow growing the roots will not fill the large container quickly enough, while quick-growing plants tend to produce too much foliage and not enough flowers and fruit.

◀ *Agapanthus lilies make good container plants with a colour range from white to deep blue. They usually need staking.*

REPOTTING

Large raised beds, especially when they contain permanent trees or shrubs, cannot easily be emptied. What you must do in these cases is remove as much of the top compost as possible and replace it with fresh compost and add a balanced fertiliser, such as Growmore. In smaller containers the compost should be emptied and replaced every other year, or every year when the plant is growing well.

Remove the plant from the container and shake the root system clear of old compost, put the plant in a bucket of water for an hour or more, then follow the planting steps above. When repotting you can tease out the root system and trim away any damaged roots.

planting – general tips

As a general rule planting in container gardens can be done at almost any time of the year. Autumn is still preferred but if you do repot in high summer, make sure that the plant is kept really moist to start with so that the roots have the best chance to grow into the new compost.

Planting bare-root trees and shrubs

There are some plants that do better, even in containers, if they are planted as bare-root specimens in the autumn. This particularly applies to roses and fruit trees. Order your roses for autumn delivery from a reputable rose grower and plant them out when you receive them. They make better plants than container-grown roses bought and planted in the spring. The same goes for fruit trees. Try and choose a specialist nursery that is used to sending specimens through the post. It is best to buy one-year-old trees as bare-root plants, or at a pinch two-year-old trees (the latter take time to become established and are more difficult to train).

▶ *Small apple trees can be grown quite happily in containers. Use John Innes No. 3 compost and feed them regularly.*

PLANTING BULBS

Bulbs absorb their strength through their foliage so never cut it off after flowering – let it yellow and fade naturally. Although this may mean untidy containers, you will get better flowering results in the long run. One solution to the straggly leaves, if cost be no object, is to throw them all away and plant new bulbs each year. If you only have room for one container of bulbs, try planting a number of different ones in layers, one below the other. All bulbs should be planted two and a half times their depth – plant the largest daffodil, *Narcissus*, bulbs at the bottom of the container with smaller crocuses and chionodoxa on top. The bulbs will grow up through each layer and flower one after the other.

planting bulbs

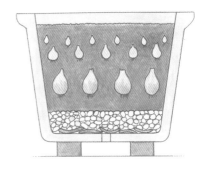

1 Put a good layer of gravel in the bottom of the container to aid drainage before starting to plant the bulbs. Use specially prepared bulb fibre.

2 Plant the largest bulbs first. Space them out evenly but put them closer together than you would if you were planting them in open ground.

3 Plant them in layers as shown above. After flowering, any bulbs grown in containers can be planted out in the garden for the following year.

Planting vines

Vines can be grown in containers, and bare-root specimens should be planted in winter when they are dormant. Add a good quantity of Growmore and make

sure that the vine is well watered during the initial growing period. Vines bought as container-grown specimens can be potted on from one container to another at any time before growth starts. Be sure that you have erected a suitable framework of wires and posts up which the vines can be trained.

Planting annuals and small bedding plants

When planting small annuals take care that the roots are not damaged. Make sure the young plants are well watered, ease the plants out of the seed tray, and then firm the compost gently around their roots in their new container. When you have finished planting out summer annuals, water them lightly with a weak solution of liquid fertilizer.

▲ *Planting a container with pansies. Position the plants at regular intervals around the rim and firm the plants in with your fingers.*

PRICKING OUT SEEDLINGS

If you have sown your own seeds, you need to prick out the seedlings into larger containers when they have germinated. Wait until they have two pairs of leaves and then ease them out of the seed tray using a small knife or a pencil. Always hold the seedlings by the first pair of leaves (the seed leaves), and not by the stalk. Handling them in this way does not damage the plant. Harden off the seedlings by placing them outside for part of the day when they are large enough, and plant out when there are no more frosts.

feeding and maintenance

All plants require nutrients to thrive and grow. In a garden these are present naturally in the soil, but in a container this is different. Not only is the volume of the growing medium far less, but frequent watering washes the nutrients away. They need to be replaced.

▲ *An ambitious fruit and vegetable garden with a traditional strawberry pot and a raised bed. The contrasting leaf colours are most attractive.*

The basic nutrients

There are three main nutrients in all soils that are needed by all plants. Each has a different function. They are nitrogen (N), phosphorus (P) and potassium (K). Nitrogen promotes good leafy growth, phosphorus enables the plant to develop a good root system, and potassium helps the plant to produce flowers and fruit. In addition to the main nutrients there are a number of other nutrients or trace elements required by plants, such as magnesium (Mg), calcium (Ca) and manganese (Mn), but they are only required in tiny amounts and can safely be ignored by container gardeners.

Organic versus inorganic It has to be said that it is very much easier for the container gardener to use inorganic fertilizers than to rely on organic alternatives. There are two main reasons for this, availability and bulk. In a standard garden there is always room for a compost heap, and if there is a lawn, grass clippings provide the essential ingredients for organic compost. A container gardener has neither of these things, although a small wormery might be a possibility, feeding the worms on suitable kitchen waste.

Compost, in a garden, has two functions. It provides much of the nutrients necessary for healthy growth, but more importantly it gives any soil bulk and helps to improve the structure. Containers, filled with prepared compost, do not require such help and do not have room for the additional bulk. Inorganic alternatives are available in compact pelleted form or in bottles of liquid fertilizer. Both can be applied easily when required. The organic alternatives of bonemeal or fish, blood and bone are perfectly satisfactory but may attract unwelcome predators.

Basic steps

When putting a permanent plant in a container you should incorporate a general fertilizer. The easiest to use is Growmore, an inorganic balanced NPK formula, 7:7:7, that contains equal proportions of nitrogen, phosphorus and

feeding a plant correctly

1 When planting a shrub or tree add some bonemeal or general fertilizer, such as Growmore, to the compost. Follow the instructions on the packet.

2 Slow-release fertilizers can be added in spring in pellet form. There are various types that work in different ways. One application lasts through summer.

3 Liquid fertilizers and foliar feeds can be added when plants are watered. These should be used when the plant is in growth, and then every 2 or 3 weeks.

potassium and provides all the plant's requirements. Do not use the organic alternatives of bonemeal or fish, blood and bone if you live where there are urban foxes. They will arrive each night

and dig up your plants time after time, looking for the bones and old fish.

Vegetables, such as tomatoes, peppers or aubergines, all need high nitrogen feeds to start them into growth,

followed by a high potassium (potash) feed when the plants are bearing fruit. Tomato feed is high in potash and is excellent for all plants as well as tomatoes.

General feeding It is a good idea to apply slow-release fertilizer granules or pellets to all permanent containers at the start of each year. Follow the manufacturer's instructions. Very often plants in containers will require no additional feeding, but if the plants do show signs of wilting, they can be watered using a foliar feed absorbed through the leaves of the plant, or be given liquid fertilizer. Foliar feeds are extremely economical and effective. When using all liquid and foliar feeds be sure to follow the manufacturer's instructions carefully.

HOW TO BUILD A WORMERY

You can buy a ready-made wormery or make your own using a plastic rubbish bin with a tap to drain off excess moisture or drainage holes and collection tray. Drill air holes around the top and make sure the lid can be fastened securely. Fill the bin with 10cm/4in gravel and then put a divider (old carpet is good) on top. Add 10cm/4in of multipurpose compost and shredded newspaper, then at least 100 red brandling worms (from angling shops). Add kitchen waste in thin layers, about 5cm/2in. Cover with damp newspaper. When the food scraps are full of worms you can add more.

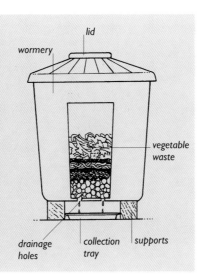

lid

wormery

vegetable waste

drainage holes

collection tray

supports

practical projects

Regularly introducing new garden features, ranging from retaining walls to trellises against a wall, to your garden is a desire of most gardeners. With careful planning, most garden projects are easily achieved, but ensure that before starting all materials are to hand, together with tools such as drills, trowels and spirit-levels. And ensure that full safety precautions are taken by using strong and secure ladders; also, protect your eyes by using clean and strong safety goggles.

creating hard surfaces

For any of a host of reasons you may want to concentrate your gardening efforts and produce a garden mainly for winter, to be enjoyed as you walk through it on your way in and out of the house, and to be viewed mainly from indoors. If so, aim to make a well-structured garden, with plenty of well-used hard materials.

Hard surfaces

If you have lengthy summer holidays away from home, or spend summer weekends walking, swimming, on your bike or down at the allotment you won't have too much time left over to admire, or work in, the garden at this time of year. Summer gardening may not be for you, so instead spend a weekend or two in the summer setting up the hard landscaping for your winter garden.

For paths and other hard surfaces it pays to buy the best materials you can afford. You can use carefully laid bricks to make various attractive features. Whatever your design, the surface is always going to be on view so good materials are worth the expense.

As for the work involved, care and attention to detail are important: laying hard surfaces takes time, but no over-demanding skills are required, and what you save by supplying your own labour you can spend on the materials. If your design has straight lines make sure they really are straight. If a geometric feature (such as our circle of

PLANTING TREES

Autumn to spring is the best time to plant. Start by digging a hole large enough to take the root-ball with space to spare for well-rotted manure and compost.

Using a stick laid across make sure the root-ball is level, then knock in the stake without damaging the roots. Add the soil, firm well with your boot, then water.

Secure the tree trunk to the stake with an adjustable tie so that the tree won't rock in the wind. Remember to check growth regularly and loosen the tie.

laying a brick path or patio

Brick paths are easily laid, but it is important to use the right kind of bricks. House bricks look attractive initially, but are unsuitable, since they tend to flake and crack in freezing weather. Use paviors, sometimes called pavers, that are specially designed for pathways, available from garden centres, DIY stores and builders' merchants.

1 Level the ground and tamp down to compact it. Cover with a layer of sharp sand, and tread this down firmly. Check the level. Set the bricks in position, butting them tightly together.

bricks) is used be sure of your geometry, and if you use curves in an informal scheme make sure the curves are pleasing (try them out using a hosepipe filled with water, doing this on a warm day, when it will be easier to manipulate).

Bricks and crazy paving need to be carefully and neatly laid but neither needs to be set in concrete. They can be laid on a level bed of sharp sand over a layer of firmly compacted, weed-free earth some 10cm/4in deep. Laying a water-permeable membrane between the earth and sand will help prevent weeds from growing through gaps.

2 Brush more sand over the surface of the bricks to fill the gaps and to prevent movement between them.

3 Place a length of strong board over the path and tamp down the bricks with a lump hammer. Brush more sand over the top to fill any remaining gaps.

planting a summer container

Once the paving has been laid, the walls painted and the screening fixed, our summer garden relies a great deal for its effect on annuals and short-lived plants, grown from seed. Container planting is also a major feature, with summer plants from pelargoniums (geraniums) to tomatoes, flowering shrubs, herbs and bulbs.

If you enjoy being in the garden on a winter's day, turning the compost heap, and catching up with jobs left over from autumn, including the digging, these are among your projects for a summer garden. You will also be justified in spending evenings in front of the fire, selecting seeds from the catalogues.

When spring comes, it's time to sow annuals as the earth warms up, and then turn your attention to containers. Buy the best you can afford, as cheap terracotta flakes in the frost and needs to be replaced, and cheap plastic looks cheap. A mixture of sizes in a limited range of types usually works better than a jumble or too many pots the same size. You will have to water at least once a day in hot, dry weather – the smaller the container, the more frequently it will need watering. Clay containers lose moisture to the air, while plastic can overheat the roots. Wooden troughs or barrels keep their contents reasonably damp, especially if lined with moss. All containers should have plenty of drainage. Be generous when planting. Three, five or seven plants of the same kind and colour in a medium-sized pot make more impact than the same number of mixed colours.

At the end of the summer remove plants that won't survive the winter and put the potting compost onto the garden or the compost heap. Clean out the container and store for winter. Alternatively, plant with winter-flowering plants or bulbs for spring. Plants which need warmth and shelter, can be brought indoors in containers.

▲ *To plant cuttings simply place them in moist compost. Cover the tray with glass or clear plastic and leave somewhere light and warm.*

DESIGNER'S TIPS

• Keep the layout simple; showy summer flowers will provide all the interest.

• Include one or two trees to provide height and dappled shade.

• Beautiful foliage is just as valuable as short-lived flowers.

• Make sure at least one-third of your plants have evergreen, bark or skeletory shape interest for quieter seasons of the year.

• Be prepared to keep on dead-heading flowers as they fade, to help prolong the flowering period.

• Fill gaps with annuals in pots or sown in situ.

• Install automatic irrigation to cope with long, dry spells.

planting a summer container

Planted up in late spring, a container can provide interest throughout the summer if you use long-flowering plants such as pelargoniums, fuchsias and bedding plants. Be sure to set them off with some reliable foliage plants, such as small-leaved ivies or the trailing *Helichrysum petiolare*.

1 Line the base of the container with crocks, pieces of broken pots or cobbles. You can further improve the drainage by adding a layer of gravel or horticultural grit.

2 Add the compost, to about two thirds of the pot's depth. You can lighten the compost by forking in perlite or vermiculite. To cut down on watering later, add water-retaining crystals.

3 Begin to plant the pot with your choice of plants. For the best effect, cram them in. Fill up around each plant with further compost. To allow for watering there should be a gap of around 250mm/1in between the top of the pot and the surface of the compost.

4 Add slow-release fertilizer. This is best applied in pelleted form in which the nutrients are released gradually throughout the summer, making further feeding unnecessary.

5 Water the container well. Water regularly throughout the summer, even if you used water-retaining crystals. Containers look best when grouped together rather than dotted singly around the garden.

building a low retaining wall

Many of the features of an easy-reach garden can be adapted to any garden, and can be borrowed by people who want to make gardening easy for themselves. Nothing in our garden sacrifices the pleasures of a garden to convenience, yet still makes an attractive, low-maintenance space.

Making things easy

Designing for people who for one reason or another have restricted movement and who want to be able to garden at elbow height need not be a problem. Raised beds have many advantages, you would probably need to employ a specialist to build a stone or brick raised planting bed. However, it is fairly simple to make a long-lasting wooden one, following the instructions given on the opposite page.

You will need to give some thought to paths and changes of level. Many people find it more difficult to handle steep steps or sudden changes of level, so keep all steps broad and shallow and avoid steep slopes by introducing terracing if necessary, with a series of broad, level areas between short flights of shallow steps. For a wheelchair user install a ramp wherever possible. They need to be able to manoeuvre themselves about freely, so keep paths wide, avoiding sharp corners or awkward changes of direction. Likewise, keep path surfaces smooth and clear of obstacles.

PRACTICAL FEATURES FOR THE GARDEN

A simple rope provides guidance for those with limited vision, or a means of balance for anyone who is no longer confident on their feet.

Raised beds at seat height allow for relaxed gardening. Wheelchair users would also benefit from a low wall they can comfortably reach over.

A gentle curving path with even, smooth slabs and no planting between lawn and path, is an ideal design for wheelchairs users as it allows them to manoevre with ease.

building a low retaining wall

You do not need bricklaying skills to make a raised bed if you opt for reclaimed railway sleepers. Check before you buy, however. Some have been treated with tar that can leach into the soil and harm your plants. Look out for new oak sleepers instead, which will not cause any problems.

1 Pile up the sleepers to the desired height, interlocking them at the corners. Drive a stake into the ground in the inside corners.

2 Screw the stakes to the sleepers, using long, rust-proof screws.

3 To prevent excess moisture entering the sleepers from the soil, line the inside of the bed with heavy-duty plastic, nailed in position with rust-proof nails. Fill the bed with soil and plant up.

◀ *A low retaining wall can look wonderful in old brick. The accompanying brick steps are shallow and wide for ease of use.*

building a scented seat

▲ *There are many types of scented seats; this one has been carefully clipped into shape and surrounded by climbing roses.*

▲ *How better to relax and enjoy the sunshine than on a scented recliner? Simply grow a bed of thyme in the shape required – then lie back!*

To be complete, a scented garden will need a scented seat. This should be located where you will get a view over a large part of the garden, while some of it is still tantalizingly hidden, to give the illusion there is yet more to be enjoyed.

A scented seat

The smell of box adds a cool, green note to a scented garden, and clipped box makes a lovely, rather architectural surround for a garden seat. As an alternative, you can create an informal scented seat in a covered arbour, made from a kit – or from your own design if you are sufficiently resourceful. Planted with climbing roses, jasmine or honeysuckle this will give perfumed shade.

If you have the patience you can make a seat from an earth bank, solidly compacted and planted with thyme or chamomile. But such seats, though most romantic, are in truth fragile. Far better is to build a seat into the retaining wall of a raised flower bed and use ordinary cushions for comfort. The scent of the herbs or flowers you use in the bed will still be released as you sit among the plants.

You can also import a stone or wooden seat, make a back for it with box or other clipped shrubs in beds or containers and grow beautifully scented plants in boxes at either end.

▲ *For artful simplicity, a rustic wooden seat is placed inside an arbour draped with beautiful scented leaves and flowers.*

Any ordinary garden bench can be made to look like a more permanent feature and incorporated into the garden by having a living alcove made around it in this way. You will need to maintain the seating area by trimming back plants neatly and regularly.

building a scented seat

Filling a planter with low-growing scented and aromatic plants is a quick and easy way to concentrate perfume in the garden. If you position the planter near a garden seat or bench you can be sure of having fragrance to enjoy whenever you take a break from your labours. Painting the planter to match the seat makes it blend with the scheme.

1 Before you fill your planter with anything, paint or stain it to match your seat. Make sure you use a plant-friendly product.

2 To make the planter watertight, line with heavy-duty polythene. Cut the polythene to fit around the top and staple it in position. Punch holes at the bottom for drainage.

BOUNDARIES FOR SCENTED GARDENS

Ideal boundaries are old, warm and mellow brick or stone walls, against which scented climbers can be trained.

Most of us don't enjoy this luxury so use 1.8m/6ft trellis battened to your fence supports.

Grow an aromatic hedge to border your scented garden. *Rosmarinus*, 'Miss Jessup's Upright', or the slow growing *Buxus sempervirens* will make hedges up to 1.2m/4ft high.

3 Plant with your selected plants. Here we used thyme and lavender. A top-dressing of grit looks attractive and improves drainage.

4 Brushing your hand gently over the plants, particularly in hot weather, will release their distinctive aroma.

73

planting a box hedge

Hedging is a useful feature in many types of garden and a dense evergreen hedge will always add a formal touch and provide structure. A low hedge can be used to divide one part of the garden from another and a high hedge is a perfect way of concealing the 'hard work' area of the garden from view.

An evergreen hedge

Box (*Buxus sempervirens*) is *the* plant for a traditional low evergreen hedge. It is ideal for a shady garden as the leaves can lose their strong green colour if the light

is too strong. We use it to make a neat dwarf hedge to enclose areas of looser planting.

If your budget can run to it, buying young plants is the best way to start as establishing a hedge is a long-term project without the additional wait for cuttings to take root. However, it is possible to grow a temporary 'hedge' using other plants (such as the annual summer cypress, *Kochia scoparia)* while you produce your own box plants, and growing plants from cuttings is very satisfying. So if you know someone whose box hedge needs trimming, step in and volunteer to help.

The best time to take cuttings is late summer, when the new growth is just beginning to ripen and become more woody. When taking cuttings the aim is not to let the plant material dry out. Therefore it's best to do it on a dull, damp day, and to keep the cuttings in a

plastic bag as you cut them. Cut off lengths up to 30cm/12in long, if possible taking them from side shoots. When you have enough, trim the cuttings to the same length, just below a leaf joint, and dip the cut ends into hormone rooting powder. Plant in pots or cutting compost or in a reserved area in the garden. You will need to add horticultural sand to the soil and cover the cutting with cloches if you strike them in the garden.

◄ *There are many types of tools available for trimming box hedge, including shears, secateurs and clippers. Ask your garden centre for advice.*

DESIGNER'S TIPS

• Don't fight dense, dry shade – just accept that very few plants will thrive there. Try *Dryopteris filix-mas* (male fern), *Euphorbia robbiae* or *Vinca minor*. If there are lots of surface roots, reveal them and put gravel around them to make them a decorative feature in their own right.

• Use yellows and whites to brighten shady corners. *Euonymus japonica, Aureovariegatus* and *Euonymus fortunei* 'Silver Queen' are excellent colourful shrubs for shade.

planting a box hedge

An evergreen hedge needs to be very carefully planted and maintained because its success depends on its formal quality. Planting lines should be marked with strings attached to pegs and the plants are normally spaced about 30cm/12in apart for a taller hedge of about 60cm/2ft high, and only 15cm/6in apart for a dwarf hedge. The hedge needs to be trimmed two to three times a year to keep it looking immaculate.

1 Mark the line of the hedge with a string stretched taut and attached to pegs driven into the ground. Dig a trench along the string.

2 Set the plants in the trench at the appropriate distance from each other and firm them in. Water well, then water daily until the plants are established and growing strongly.

CLIPPING A BOX HEDGE

Box responds well to clipping, which produces a sheer surface of tight, dense growth. Unless you have a very good eye, it can be a good idea to run a horizontal line at the height you wish to trim the hedge.

Box can be trimmed with shears, secateurs or the special clippers shown here. Hold the blades as near flush to the surface as possible. Be sure to trim wayward shoots right back. Trim in spring and mid- to late summer.

sowing meadow seed

To achieve a meadow haze you will need to become adept at raising plants from seed. But most meadow plants are either long-lived perennials or else self-seeding annuals, so once you have done the groundwork your garden should work for you. Seeds are available as named meadow or wild flower varieties and in mixes.

Easy sowing

Most suitable meadow plants can be grown easily from seed, and this is generally the best way to grow plants needed in such large quantities. Some seeds have to be sown directly into the ground as the young plants don't like to be disturbed, while others, such as the meadow cranesbill in our garden, can be started in seed trays and planted out into position as young plants. Seedlings always need light and warmth as well as moisture once they are growing, which means that seeds are generally sown outside only when the earth has warmed up, and the ground needs to be well watered unless it's been raining. Like the grass in our meadow, seeds specifically sold as meadow mixtures are normally sown direct into the ground.

Individual plants

For accent plants, a very good alternative is to buy plug plants, which have been germinated and started off in ideal conditions. These are potted on into larger pots before being planted out in their chosen positions. Grown in this way they benefit from not having their roots disturbed when being moved on. Primrose, harebell, red campion, cowslip, ox-eye daisy and cornflower are some of the meadow plants frequently available, and of course you can grow your own seedlings in the same way. Which will give you an even wider choice.

BROADCAST SOWING

For any meadow mixture, prepare the ground as you would for a lawn, except that no fertilizer should be added.

Rake over the surface to make it smooth and level. Scatter the seed by hand. Water in with a fine sprinkler.

sowing meadow seed

If you want more control over the final result than can be achieved by broadcast sowing, as described on page 76, sow individual types of seed according to their specific requirements. Remember that germination rates vary depending on the species, and some will self-seed freely, so that the meadow will never look the same two years in succession.

1 Prepare the ground as normal, but add no supplementary fertilizer. For larger seeds, make shallow trenches with a trowel.

2 For smaller seeds, mark rills in the soil with a hoe. Some seed can be surface sown.

3 Sow the seed thinly. For large seed, allow a space of about 1cm/½in in between seeds. Mix fine seed with sand. Gently draw the soil over the seeds. Thin seedlings once they have germinated.

4 By summer, the meadow will be a sea of colour. The majority of meadow plants will self-seed, and over the course of the years the species best suited to the site will predominate.

borders and staking plants

Planning the shape and content of the borders is one of the chief projects for this garden, bearing in mind the plants' height, size, shape and colour. Once you have got your designs worked out on paper, trace them in on the ground to see how they will fit and then have fun getting the plants together.

Planting schemes

The aim is to arrange the plants you choose for the border so that there will always be something at its best to take over as other plants fade, to keep them going for the longest possible period. Generous curves can be made on the ground using a length of rope and a peg as a radius. A general principle is to have taller plants at the back and shorter at the front, but not in a regimented way.

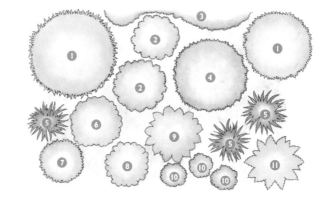

1. Aucuba japonica 'Salicifolia'
2. Thalictrum rochebruneanum
3. Hedera helix 'Glacier'
4. Viburnum tinus
5. Phormium tenax
6. Saxifraga hirsuta
7. Epimedium
8. Trillium grandiflorum
9. Hosta crispula
10. Viola odorata
11. Athyrium filix-femina

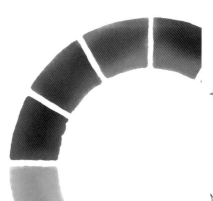

▲ *Colour is a key aspect of design. Opposite colours tend to blend well, while neighbouring colours work less well together.*

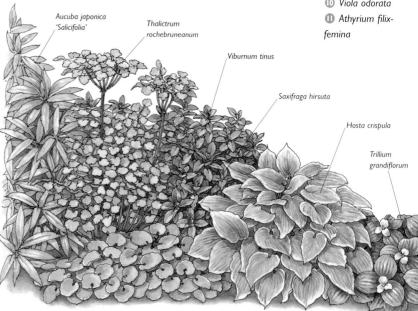

Aucuba japonica 'Salicifolia'

Thalictrum rochebruneanum

Viburnum tinus

Saxifraga hirsuta

Hosta crispula

Trillium grandiflorum

staking plants

Many tall border perennials benefit from staking, particularly those with heavy heads of flowers that can easily flop over, such as peonies or delphiniums. The traditional method is with pea sticks or rods of hazel, and these have the advantage of being unobtrusive once the plants have grown to cover them.

◀ *A shady border – plan from above and as a cross-section.*

1 In early to mid-spring, cut lengths of branching, twiggy hazel (pea sticks) up to 1.2m/4ft long using sharp secateurs.

2 Drive the hazel sticks into the soil around the plants, arching them inwards, and burying them up to one third of their length.

3 Unless the sticks are very twiggy, it may be necessary to tie the plant stems loosely to them as they grow, with wire, horticultural twine or raffia. Once the plant has reached flowering size, tie in any loose stems.

AN ALTERNATIVE METHOD OF STAKING

Proprietary link stakes are available in garden centres and by mail order and are usually made of metal coated with green plastic. These stakes have the advantage over pea sticks in that they can be used year on year and are more readily available. The fresh growth will soon hide them from view.

At the start of the growing season, insert the uprights in the ground around the plant, pushing them deep into the soil so that the horizontal members support the emerging growth. As the plant grows, gradually raise the stakes until there is enough support against wind damage.

Ring stakes have a circular horizontal disc with a coarse mesh through which the plant stems grow. This type is suitable for plants with tall, thin stems.

creating a garden wigwam

True cottagers grew plants mainly for practical purposes, using every inch of space available. Whether or not the plants are to be used, the cottage garden look is still very much in fashion. A multitude of plants of all kinds flourish at close quarters and all you need are plant supports and somewhere to walk.

Minimal skill required

Maintaining a cottage garden will require quite a bit of skill and hard work, but the skills involved in putting it together are not beyond the reach of anyone who can manage a few simple tools. Cottage gardens need frequent titivating, so good access is required, and every available bit of space is used for plants – including the vertical.

A freestanding support for climbing plants is useful if you don't have suitable walls or fences, or have already covered them with plants. It makes a decorative, semi-permanent feature to give the garden some structural interest during the winter months when the soil is mostly bare.

The most stable support is wider at its base than at the top and a wigwam shape is ideal as it is unlikely to topple over in strong winds. Straight hazel poles, willow withies, or simple, thick bamboo poles are all equally suitable.

To make a natural looking walkway over the grass, set weather-proofed railway sleepers or lengths of pressure-treated timber into the lawn or gravel surface.

◄ *When plants are grown closely together, they support each other to some extent and less staking is therefore needed.*

DESIGNER'S TIPS

• Buy a Dutch hoe. You'll need it to remove unwanted seedlings that will spring up everywhere.

• Don't lay fine shingle if you own a cat. It makes a wonderful litter tray!

• Stake tall plants with blue, pink, or red painted bamboo canes, for protection and added colour.

creating a wigwam

Choose a level site for the wigwam, and clear the ground of weeds. Decide how tall you want it to be, then add one half again to determine the length of the individual poles. This is to allow for the slope of the poles and the amount to be buried in the ground for stability.

1 To mark the position of the outer poles, drive a pole into the centre of the prepared area and tie some string to it. Mark out a circle, about 1m/3ft across.

2 Cut a piece of weed-suppressing membrane to the size of the wigwam at the base, make a hole in the centre, and slip it over the central pole. Weigh it down with a layer of gravel, shingle or cobbles.

3 Drive the stakes into the ground around the perimeter of the circle, bending them inwards. Secure them about 30cm/12in from the top with string or wire. Wind rounds of wire or flexible cane at regular intervals up the wigwam.

LAYING A TIMBER PATH

First decide on the position of each timber. Stand on the timber to prevent it moving, and cut along the edge all round with a sharp half-moon edger.

Remove the turf and line the base of the trench with a thin layer of cement. Lay the timber on top.

Tamp down the timber, making sure it is flush with the lawn. When you have finished, check the level with a spirit level.

lining a bog garden

A bog or damp garden is easily made using flexible lining material and makes a lovely, informal water feature. Bog areas can link a pond to the rest of the garden but they can also form a feature in their own right.

▲ Primula vialii *is a hardy perennial.*

Bogs in nature aren't a feature of open, sunny places, so you need to site this kind of garden thoughtfully. If you haven't made a pond near which a damp garden will be sited, the most natural looking place will be in a hollow (existing or dug out) in a low-lying part of the garden, preferably where there is some shade.

You are aiming to create an area that is constantly moist, yet where there is enough movement of air through the soil to prevent it from becoming stagnant and provide plant roots with oxygen. When constructed next to a pond the bog garden will absorb some overspill water, but if it is self-contained you will need to top it up in dry weather.

All you do is to make a hollow of a suitable depth and shape and line it with perforated pond liner. A bottom layer of gravel will help drainage, while clean soil and a gravel top-dressing form the planting medium.

▼ *This cross-section shows how a bog garden can be created using simple materials. This will enable damp-loving plants to flourish.*

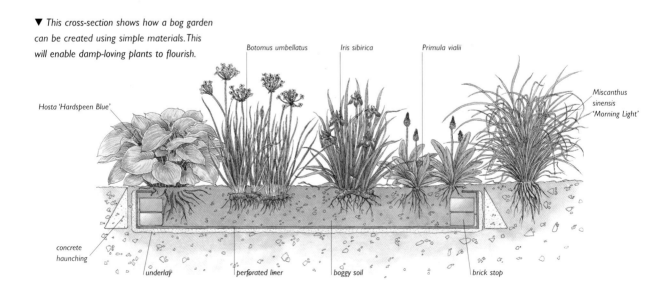

Hosta 'Hardspeen Blue'

Botomus umbellatus

Iris sibirica

Primula vialii

Miscanthus sinensis 'Morning Light'

concrete haunching

underlay

perforated liner

boggy soil

brick stop

lining a bog

The aim in making an artificial bog garden is to slow down the rate at which water drains through the soil – easily achieved with a perforated impermeable liner. This will allow you to grow a range of plants that thrive in permanently moist ground. Some added drainage is essential, however, if the soil is not to become stagnant.

DESIGNER'S TIPS

• Make sure the level of the water table will not be higher than the bottom of the new pond or bog garden, especially if you use a flexible liner.

• Don't introduce fish to a pond or plants to a pond or bog garden until at least one week after, so that any chemicals in the tap water can disperse.

• Add lots of oxygenating plants – better to have too many and remove some occasionally than too few.

• For moving water features install a pump that is powerful enough to circulate the water effectively. Your supplier will advise you on pump capacities if you supply your pond dimensions.

• Never try to create a bog garden or a pond on high ground. It will look unnatural and it will be hard to maintain adequate moisture levels.

• Don't choose vigorous plants, for example bulrush, for a small garden – they will take over. Some grasses, such as *Phalaris arundinacea* and *Carex pendula* are also very invasive.

1 Dig a hole the area of the proposed bog garden. Depending on the ultimate size of the plants you wish to grow, this can be up to 1m/3ft in depth. Remove sharp rocks that could pierce the liner and all traces of weeds.

2 Level the base of the hole and line it with a flexible rubber pond liner. Pierce holes in the liner to allow excess water to drain away.

3 Line the base with pebbles or gravel. (Avoid limestone chippings if you wish to grow acid-loving plants.) Fill with clean garden soil.

4 Flood the area with water prior to planting. You may find it necessary to water the bog generously during prolonged periods of hot, dry weather in summer.

water garden features

Water features look sophisticated but are relatively simple to install. They can be bought complete and ready made or you can buy a submersible pump and devise something of your own imagining, with water trickling from a wall spout or welling from the ground.

▲ *A reproduction antique drinking fountain is an ideal feature for an enclosed courtyard garden, nestling among climbing plants.*

DESIGNER'S TIPS

• If you raise your submersible pump by standing it on bricks you are less likely to suck debris into it.

• Either bring in your pump during the winter, or make sure that you use it for at least an hour once a week to keep it in good order.

• If you have a pump with a filter clean this out regularly.

• **ALWAYS CALL A QUALIFIED ELECTRICIAN TO INSTALL A PUMP.**

Small water features

Water features must be beautiful of course, but for most of us they also need to be simple to install and maintain. The under-stated is more successful than the over-ambitious and the design should suit the immediate garden surroundings in scale and style. There are plenty of different designs to choose from.

Naturally you need access to an electricity supply, with a length of armoured cable and a waterproof connector to connect to the pump. The cable from the supply, protected with armoured sleeving, must be safely buried at least 60cm/2ft below the soil surface, and you should always use a residual current device (trip switch) fitted to the socket, to break the circuit if anything goes wrong. The pump should be completely submerged and will be connected to the water feature with flexible plastic piping.

A 24-volt pump should be a satisfactory strength for a small feature, with a transformer to adapt the mains supply. This lives inside the house.

▲ *This traditional wall fountain is in a classical style, and would certainly add interest to any terrace or patio.*

▶ *A bubble fountain erupts from the centre of an old mill wheel surrounded by cobbles that conceal the reservoir.*

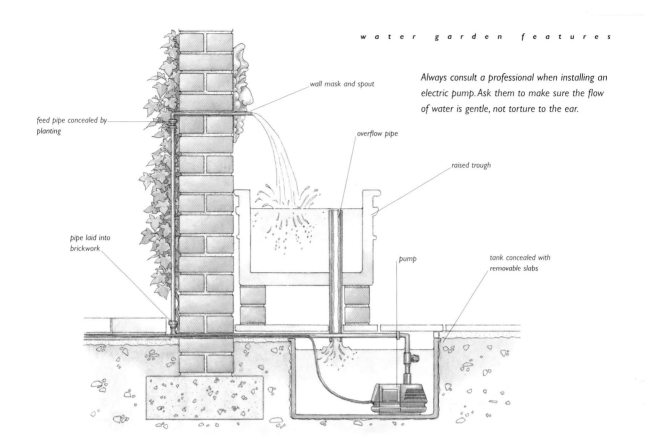

feed pipe concealed by planting

wall mask and spout

Always consult a professional when installing an electric pump. Ask them to make sure the flow of water is gentle, not torture to the ear.

overflow pipe

raised trough

pipe laid into brickwork

pump

tank concealed with removable slabs

erecting a trellis against a wall

Trellis battened to a wall makes a useful framework for many plants. Whatever you intend to grow, make sure that the trellis is fixed just clear of the wall to allow air to flow. In a herb garden it can be used to support nasturtiums (whose leaves, flowers and fruits are edible), hops, blackberries and ornamental fruit.

Support and shelter

One of the skills involved in creating a herb garden is to appreciate, and provide, the conditions herbs require. Most herbs (like most vegetables) need warmth and good light, and don't enjoy wind. Providing shelter will be necessary if you have an open position. Bamboo screens can fulfil this function while also being a

good-looking way of hiding any unsightly or purely functional parts of the garden. Although temporary, they have a lovely natural look that blends with the simple shapes and planting of the herb garden, and they are cheap and easy to replace.

If you are lucky enough to have a walled garden it will provide maximum

shelter allowing you to grow a huge array of different plants. Make optimum use of the wall by growing suitable companion plants up it. Flowering plants such as roses and climbing vegetables such as runner beans, as well as ornamental vines and fruits, can all be grown on trellis and have a natural affinity with herbs.

SCREENS AND CURTAINS

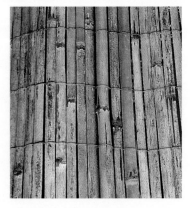

Bamboo curtains can be used to screen off rubbish bins and to separate out differen parts of the garden. These curtains can be

put to many different uses – for example in a roof garden they can be used to disguise the safety railings. Here is a selection of

some of the different thicknesses and styles that are available.

trellis against a wall

In order to grow twining climbers against walls, it is necessary to provide them with some kind of support fixed to the wall. One of the simplest methods uses ready-made trellis panels. If you are using wooden panels, make sure they have been treated with a preservative before proceeding.

1 Cut small wooden battens on which to mount the trellis and drill holes through the length of them. This avoids damage to old walls.

2 Use a masonry bit to drill holes in the wall at the appropriate intervals.

DESIGNER'S TIPS

• Trim clump-forming herbs after flowering, to avoid straggly, woody-stemmed plants.

• If you don't want your herbs to self-seed, trim before they flower. But remember you will have to replace annual herbs with new plants next year.

• Harvest herbs before they flower, in dry, but not hot, conditions.

• Herbs with variegated leaves may be less hardy than those of single colour foliage.

• Chamomile lawns usually get untidy and weedy very quickly; avoid them.

• Don't experiment with herbal remedies or use them in cooking without reading instructions. Some herbs are very poisonous.

• Beware of rue. It can give you nasty blisters when handled.

• If you have heavy, clay soil, grow your herbs in raised beds.

3 Tap in Rawlplugs to hold the screws. Place the battens in position so that the holes in the battens line up with the holes in the wall.

4 Using long screws, screw the trellis to the wall through the battens. Using battens (rather than fixing the trellis directly to the wall) allows for good air circulation behind the plant.

constructing a trellis

A courtyard garden is defined by its enclosures. You may be lucky enough to have a ready-made area adjoining the house, but if not, a sturdy, well-supported trellis makes a quick and straight-forward enclosure and shelter from winds.

▲ *This wood trellis permits a glimpse through to another part of the garden and allows the garden to have different components to it.*

Making an enclosure

A courtyard garden is a garden on a small scale, where everything is visible at close quarters. It also has a degree of formality that comes from being closely attached to the house, and is an area where you will be sitting and looking around much of the time. For all these reasons, good workmanship is especially important.

Since a large part of the effect will come from plants growing up the enclosure, anything you build needs to be strong enough to take the weight of plants climbing or twining over it, and also sufficiently well finished to make sure that it will wear well.

If you use ready-made trellis panels, choose the strongest available and fix them between strong posts. For easy fixing as well as long life, special metal post holders can be used. Trellis looks good painted to go with the house or with other features. Dark garden green

forms a restful background to plants and French grey is a calming colour. If you prefer the look of natural, bare wood, protect with wood seal. Or you could be adventurous and choose a bright colour, to contrast with the colour of any flowers or green foliage. Paints, seals and varnishes are all available in non-toxic, water-based formulas.

◀ *The delicate white and purple flowers of Clematis 'Sieboldii' complement this trellis. It is an especially good climber.*

DESIGNER'S TIPS

• Choose hard landscaping materials that complement or match the materials of your house.

• Don't try to create a Mediterranean hotspot if the courtyard is exposed to wind or cold.

• Don't choose a shady and dry area for your courtyard. Unless you use an automatic irrigation system the plants will die and you'll be left with a brown dustbowl. If it's cool it needs to be damp and that may not suit your purpose.

• Decide on a single, main theme for your courtyard: don't have too many ideas crammed into its small space.

• The higher the boundaries, the more shady your courtyard will be.

putting up trellis

Trellis panels are easily erected, but if they are to be a lasting feature in the garden, it is worth taking the trouble to put them up correctly. Good fence posts will carry a guarantee of 15 years or longer. The panels are fixed to timber uprights firmly anchored in the ground. These can either be cemented in or held in place by means of the foundation posts illustrated here. Most fencing materials sold today have already been pressure treated to make them weatherproof, but check before you buy.

1 Check the position of the uprights carefully, making sure they are the correct distance from each other and that they are square on to each other.

2 Drive the foundation posts well into the ground, using a lump hammer and a wooden block.

3 Knock the uprights into the metal shoes and bolt them in firmly. Use a spirit level to make sure that the post is upright.

4 Screw the panels to the uprights, using rust-proof metal plates.

5 Fix finials to the tops of the posts. Not only are these decorative in their own right, but they will deflect rain that would otherwise collect at the top of the post and cause rotting.

building a rose arch

A timber arch for climbing roses is a traditional rose garden feature, and simple arches are useful to give height and a sense of structure in many garden situations. As well as enabling you to grow climbing plants they can also frame a focal point, or allow you to separate your garden into a series of different spaces.

Framing the scene

In every size of plot attention to scale and form brings balance to the scheme. Luckily, what is comfortable for the human figure also generally delights the human eye.

An arch has to be tall and wide enough for practical purposes. For example, using posts that are 3m/9ft long produces a 2m-/7ft-high opening when driven 60cm/2ft into the ground. This will allow the roses to tumble down naturally and prettily while still leaving room for the tallest visitor to walk comfortably underneath. An opening width of 1.2m/4ft, will be nicely in balance with this height and allow plenty of room for people to walk through without getting entangled with the thorny stems. It will also mean that there is no problem for two friendly people to walk side by side, and space for pushing a wheelbarrow or lawn mower through the arch.

A log roll can be used to make an attractive border edge. These logs can be set at different heights, allowing you to create a raised border and they are ideal for a curved bed. See the panel below for full instructions.

LAYING LOG ROLL

Log roll is one of the most versatile materials for edging beds, borders and pathways, as it is flexible and can be curved in any shape you may choose. Most has already been treated. Decide how much of the edging you wish to protrude above ground level and dig a trench. Place the roll in position and, with a mallet, tap it into place, checking the level with a spirit level. Back fill any gaps with garden soil and firm down.

building a rose arch

A timber arch makes a charming support for climbing or rambling roses and is easily made. Use chesnut, birch or thich bamboo poles. When measuring up, you need to allow at least 60cm/2ft of timber below ground for maximum stability. A height of 2.2m/7ft and a width of 1.2m/4ft will allow most adults to pass through without rose thorns catching on their clothing. For our garden we used four uprights each with three bracers and two 1.8m/6ft poles along the top, again with three bracers. The two uprights were constructed first, followed by the top section.

1 For ease of work, lay the timbers on the ground and mark on the verticals the position of the horizontal cross pieces. Chisel out cross-halving joints at the appropriate points, so that the beams will fit together.

2 Fit the posts together and screw or nail them in place. Depending on the roses' habit of growth, you may need more cross pieces than shown here.

3 Assemble the horizontal top section and fix it in place with long screws.

4 Dig trenches in the ground to the appropriate depth (60cm/2ft is recommended) and insert the finished arch. Use a spirit level or a plumb line to make sure it is absolutely vertical.

DESIGNER'S TIPS

• Don't have too many fragrant roses in a garden – the mixed scents can be almost overpowering on a still day.

• Add companion plants to soften the woody base of the rose plants and to add variety of texture and form.

• Use bent hazel or willow wands to anchor and contain rose beds – they look gentler than stakes or canes.

building a seaside windbreak

The soil is almost always poor in coastal areas, and you are often faced with exposed and windy conditions, even if there is sun. Design to face these challenges by making over a large area to a timber-floored dining and sitting space and building a wooden palisade to act as a windbreak.

A nautical air

In a seaside garden you may enjoy seafood barbecues, do some undisturbed sun worshipping, and take advantage of the local micro-climate to grow something exotic and unusual without having to spend too much time coaxing unwilling plants.

Building a palisade fence will help to turn a sunny coastal plot into a more sheltered seaside garden, making it more conducive to planting and to sitting despite the otherwise exposed situation – the perfect place for growing sun-loving plants and basking in the sun.

This sort of windbreak has a homespun look and there is no need to worry about careful measuring. An uneven top to the fence ties in with the garden's rustic furniture and sleeper decking. The decking laid directly into shingle gives a nautical look and the theme is continued throughout. Controlled irregularity is the look you are aiming for and constructing out of natural materials, preferably from the area or seashore, for that weathered look.

DESIGNER'S TIPS

• Remember it is illegal to remove stones, boulders, pebbles or cobbles from their natural setting.

• Try to use only native plants and local materials. Anything alien to your seascape will look just that.

• Position driftwood, boulders and plants to lie directionally along the invisible line of the prevailing wind and weather.

• Gauge the direction of weather fronts from the way that surrounding shrubs and trees grow to lean away from the wind.

◀ *Seaside dwellers are bound to have lots of visitors, so these gardens benefit from an area for entertaining and feeding that sea appetite.*

building a rustic seaside windbreak

A rustic-looking windbreak is easily made. If you live by the sea, the timbers will soon weather attractively, but if you garden inland but want that distinctive seaside look, try staining them to the appropriate bleached colour – a soft whitish grey is best.

1 Dig a trench to a depth of up to a third the length of the longest piece of timber.

2 Line the base of the trench with pebbles or coarse gravel for good drainage around the base of the timbers.

3 Cut the timbers to length. For a really rustic look, make sure the lengths are uneven. Stain the timbers if you feel it necessary.

4 Knock the timbers well into the ground using a mallet and a piece of timber held horizontally over the top.

5 Leave a gap between each timber to help filter the wind. The uneven topline will break the wind further and look less rigid.

index

PICTURE CREDITS:
Liz Eddison, Designers: Christopher Costin 70bl, br; Julian Doyle fc; Gavin Landscaping 47; Angela Mainwaring 70bc; Peter McHoy fcb, 43tl, tr, bl, br; Natural & Oriental Water Garden 46b; Judith Sharpe 92; Wynniatt-Husey Clark 11t. Hozelock 32b, r. Harry Smith Collection 24b, 25, 31, 42, 36r. Spear & Jackson 14, 15; David Squire 21, 26bl.